D1738143

PURCHASED WITH NEH
ENDOWMENT FUNDS

LOUISE BOGAN'S
AESTHETIC OF
LIMITATION

LOUISE BOGAN'S AESTHETIC OF LIMITATION

GLORIA BOWLES

INDIANA UNIVERSITY PRESS
BLOOMINGTON AND INDIANAPOLIS

For my mother and father,
Catherine Janes Bowles and George Edward Bowles

Manufactured in the United States of America

Library of Congress Cataloging-in-Publication Data

Bowles, Gloria.
Louise Bogan's aesthetic of limitation.

Bibliography: p.
Includes index.
1. Bogan, Louise, 1897–1970—Criticism and
interpretation.   2. Feminism and literature—
United States.   I. Title.
PS3503.0195Z55   1987   811'.52   86-45954
ISBN 0-253-33602-3

1 2 3 4 5 91 90 89 88 87

I might have sung of the world
  And said what I heard them say
Of the vast and passing dream
  Of today and yesterday.

But I chose to tell of myself,
  For that was all I knew—
I have made a chart of a small sea,
  But the chart I made is true.

—Sara Teasdale, 1919

Woman, economic, perfectionist causes—
all inextricably intertwined.

—Tillie Olsen, *Silences*

CONTENTS

ACKNOWLEDGMENTS

I am indebted to the many friends who supported this work, which has been a long time coming; it got pushed to the back burner, as I coordinated and taught in the Women's Studies program at Berkeley for nine years. My own work has been enriched by the emergence of the new feminist criticism which is establishing a specific tradition of women's poetry. My thinking owes a great deal to Susan Stanford Friedman for her monumental work on H.D.; to Sandra Gilbert and Susan Gubar for their paradigms of women's writing; to Suzanne Juhasz, one of the first to think in terms of "women's poetry"; to Cheryl Walker for her lucid and comprehensive insights into our legacy; to Jaqueline Ridgeway for her studies of Bogan; to Diane Wood Middlebrook, who is a model as poet, scholar, and feminist. It is one of the marks of feminist knowledge that these women scattered over the country became not just colleagues but also friends. I attribute the rapid growth of our scholarship in part to the kinds of non-competitive collaborations which we have shared.

Students in the Women's Studies programs where I have taught, at Berkeley, Stanford, and Davis, have been a constant source of challenge and insight. I wish especially to thank Daphne Beletsis, Jennifer McNulty, Colette Patt, Mary Lautzenhiser, Sarah Lutes, Joanne Ring, and Taly Rutenberg. My seminars on Bogan with undergraduates at Berkeley offered new perspectives; I watched with amazement, and then gratitude, as these young women and men found in Bogan wisdom for their own lives. One of them had the profound insight that "the lack of knowledge and concern for women's writing is one of the fundamental reasons why it's been so difficult for women to write"—and thus gave me new reasons to keep on with my work.

Barbara Christian and Thalia Kitrilakis read many versions of this manuscript even as they pursued their own writing. Eric Mills did more than type manuscripts; he also read my words. Susan Peabody read a final draft of the manuscript first as critic and then with care as an editor. Renate Duelli-Klein has been a close friend and collaboratrice, first with *Theories of Women's Studies* and then the *Women's Studies International Forum* and the Athene Series published by Pergamon Press. The staff and faculty of Special Programs at Berkeley worked with me intelligently and supportively; these include Marty Gaetjens, Jane Hutzell, Greg Martin, Dean William B. Slottman, and Deborah Towle.

I am very grateful for the many friends and colleagues who have believed in my work over the last decade; they include Dorothy Brown, Patricia Cooper, Sandra Coyner, Phyllis Hall, Judith Harris, Elaine Kaplan, Mary Jo Lakeland, Robin Lakoff, Nancy Lindsley, Anne Machung, Michele Mills, Maresi Nerad, Deborah Rosenfelt, Rena Rosenwasser, Dale Spender, Judith Stacey, Elizabeth

Thomsen, and Frances Van Loo. I have been greatly enriched by friendships with talented younger scholars of women's poetry who will continue our work, especially Mary De Shazer and Susan Schweik. And I am deeply grateful to Phyllis Peacock for the renewal of friendship and my garden.

My family has also made possible my continuing commitment to a thoughtful life. The good humor and tenderness of my brothers, Franklin and Stephen, has been sustaining. The greatest gratitude goes to my parents, Catherine Janes Bowles and George Edward Bowles, whose acceptance and love and high standards have always been a source of inspiration.

I would like to thank Ruth Limmer, literary executor of Louise Bogan's estate, the Viking Press, and Farrar, Straus & Giroux, Inc., for permission to quote from Bogan's writings, both published and unpublished. Permission was granted by Macmillan Publishing Co. to quote the poetry of Sara Teasdale from *Mirror of the Heart* (New York, 1984). The Collection of American Literature, the Beinecke Rare Book and Manuscript Library of Yale University, gave permission to quote from the H.D. Papers (Marianne Moore to H.D., October 29, 1944).

LOUISE BOGAN'S AESTHETIC OF LIMITATION

INTRODUCTION
THE AESTHETIC OF LIMITATION

> All art, in spite of the struggles of some
> critics to prove otherwise, is based on
> emotion and projects emotion.
>
> —Louise Bogan, *Journey Around My Room*

> Something inheres in women's poetry which
> has the force of a secret kept alive by a
> clandestine group.
>
> —Cheryl Walker, *The Nightingale's Burden*

> The world's greatest creative artists have
> turned the hard white light of their spirits
> into the inmost recesses of even their own
> souls, and what they found there they
> recorded without subterfuge and without
> shame. And this is the thing that woman
> has not yet been able to do. From her first
> lispings, she has consciously, or uncon-
> sciously, acquired the art of concealment.
>
> —Lola Ridge, "Women and the
> Creative Will"

The Aesthetic of Limitation argues that Louise Bogan is a major modernist
poet. Louise Bogan is a modernist with a difference—she is a woman. A
formalist, she writes from female experience: Her integration of a glassy poetic
surface and female subject matter have confused formalist and feminist critics
alike. Assumptions about formalism and female subject matter have hindered
access to the critical tools that would help us understand the work of Louise
Bogan. This idea of "limitation" links form and subject matter as it suggests a
relationship: The white woman poet must define herself in terms of two
traditions, the female and the male. In Bogan's work, this negotiation led to an
"aesthetic of limitation," or a strict idea of what a woman poet could and
could not permit herself. A self-taught literary historian and the poetry critic of
the *New Yorker* for thirty-eight years, Bogan absorbed modernism's formal
lessons, using its standards of compactness and control to rein in "female
emotion"; yet her subjects were women's subjects, heterosexual love and

disillusionment and breakdown and an uneasy peace with the self. Her work is an extreme example of a woman's internalization of male ideas of the woman poet. The limits Bogan imposed on herself and the creative limits that were placed upon her are identical. Her oeuvre is contained in the 105 poems of her final collection, *The Blue Estuaries: Poems 1923–1968*. Out of this self-censorship came perfectionism and, inevitably, silence. Yet paradoxically, as she encapsulated male strictures, Bogan created a peculiarly female idiom, thus adding to and transforming the female tradition of poetry.

This book uses the methods of feminist literary criticism. I refer to biography where it is relevant and read *The Blue Estuaries* in conjunction with un-published or uncollected poems as well as short stories, journals, letters, and literary criticism. This method shows how the complex interactions of gender, a working-class background, a particular temperament, and dominant literary modes all come together to create a poetic voice. My own work was complete as the new Bogan criticism emerged, although its findings buttress my own, and I have taken them into account at relevant points. To the pioneers of feminist criticism on women's poetry I owe the deepening of my own study. Among those scholars who began establishing the existence of a female tradi-tion is Cheryl Walker, who, in *The Nightingale's Burden* (Indiana University Press, 1982) began the enormous task of tracing historically the tradition of American women's poetry. Sandra M. Gilbert and Susan Gubar's *The Mad-woman in the Attic: The Woman Writer and the Nineteenth Century Literary Imagination* (Yale University Press, 1979) has been enormously helpful to my work. In addition, their edited volume, *Shakespeare's Sisters: Feminist Essays on Women Poets* (Indiana University Press, 1979) was the first of its kind and crucial to a critical community that initially gave its attention to women's successes with the novel. Susan Stanford Friedman's ground-breaking work on H.D., *Psyche Reborn: The Emergence of H.D.* (Indiana University Press, 1981) has been a pivotal example of the excavations necessary to bring our women poets into the light of day. And the prolific work of Suzanne Juhasz, especially *Naked and Fiery Forms* (Harper & Row, 1976), has contributed immensely to defining important questions for the feminist scholar of women's poetry. It is perhaps a little odd that, in this so-called "post-modernist" age—marked by its criticisms of modernism, its sense even that it is a little old-fashioned—we are just beginning to understand the female modernist tradition. Yet only when we understand the contributions of women will we have an integrated and balanced perspective on the period which precedes our own.

Several studies, then, helped to establish some of the theoretical approaches to the study of poetry by women. Only recently have we had the biographical background that would help us to bring Louise Bogan into the canon. The various anthologies of women's poetry that came out in the early seventies also began to make the work of Bogan and others visible. When I began my work, there were the poems, that slim volume, *The Blue Estuaries;* then, in 1973, the letters appeared, edited by Ruth Limmer. Jaqueline Ridgeway finished her dissertation on Bogan in 1977. In 1980 Ruth Limmer's "mosaic" of an autobiography appeared. It is primarily to Limmer that we owe the slowly emerging record of Bogan's work. In effect, critical work on Bogan had to wait for the emergence of these autobiographical fragments. During her lifetime, Bogan was extremely reticent about self-revelation. As the new feminist criticism has taught us, we need to know something about a writer's life in order to understand her art; this is especially true for an art as difficult as Bogan's. The beginnings of a body of criticism began to emerge in 1984 and 1985. Jaqueline Ridgeway's *Louise Bogan,* published in the Twayne series (1984), was the first book. *Critical Essays on Louise Bogan,* edited by Marie Collins (G. K. Hall, 1984), republishes many of those short periodical reviews of Bogan's work that appeared over the years. It is useful to have these reviews in a single volume since some of them are remarkably acute evaluations; W. H. Auden's review of *Poems and New Poems* in 1942 is a notable example. In addition, *Critical Essays* includes several new articles that mark the beginning of a serious interest among contemporary scholars. In 1984 Deborah Pope published *A Separate Vision: Isolation in Contemporary Women's Poetry* (Louisiana State University Press), which includes a chapter on Bogan. Pope is extremely sensitive in her readings of individual poems; her book is somewhat undermined by a theme that posits a progression from Bogan, as an example of constriction, to Adrienne Rich, representative of relative freedom. The publication in early 1985 of Elizabeth Frank's biography, *Louise Bogan: A Portrait* (Knopf), was a central event. Frank's beautifully written and researched portrait, a psychological study, gives us the details of a life whose psychic outlines are hinted at in the poems.[1]

The first chapter of this book presents "Outlines of an Artist's Life" as they impinge on the work. In the second chapter, "The Authority of Male Tradition," I analyze Bogan's relationship to modernism and its precursors, focusing primarily on her readings of the symbolists and Yeats. In chapter 3, "The Lost Female Tradition," I discuss Bogan's decision to dissociate herself from the female tradition of women's poetry as she understood it, that tradition of the wailing poetess; and I point out how little of the women's literary tradition was available to her as she wrote. I chart Bogan's complicated and evolving relationship to the female tradition, and to the women writers who were her contemporaries; I document how her distancing in the early years eventually gave way to an appreciation of the "heart" that women bring to poetic endeavor. Part II, "The Achievement," establishes Bogan's place among major modernist poets, through an analysis of the dominant themes and images of *Body of This Death* (1923), *Dark Summer* (1929), and *The Sleeping Fury* (1937). I also interpret the tiny production of her later years. "The Achievement" focuses on both Bogan's expressions and her suppressions, those poems she published in small magazines and elected not to include in later editions of her work.

This book yields insights that go beyond Bogan. Literature gives us a particularly focused opportunity to see the intricate workings of what is now an emerging paradigm in the study of women—the ways in which women, whether conscious or unconscious of the constrictions of patriarchy, try to

maximize limitation. In Bogan this strategy takes the form of a severe perfectionism—the "knife of perfectionism," Tillie Olsen called it.[2] Bogan limited
herself to a slender oeuvre in part because she felt that a woman poet in her
time could be nothing less than "perfect." As feminist critics, we recognize this
perfectionism as one of the many strategies of women and women artists even
as we measure its costs. Because of her subject matter, Louise Bogan has not
been accessible to male readers and critics; and in an age when confessional
and experimental forms receive homage, her work has tended to mislead most
feminist critics and poets because she used those modernist forms to mask
content. There is perhaps yet another reason for the relative neglect of Bogan
by feminist poets and critics, an aspect even of conscious neglect. Those
anthologies of poetry by women that we welcomed in the seventies inevitably
included poems with "female" or "woman" in the title; thus, among feminists
Louise Bogan is best known for her poem "Women." And "Women," we
should not be surprised to learn, has been read as a "self-hate," and thus a
"woman-hating," poem:

> Women have no wilderness in them,
> They are provident instead,
> Content in the tight hot cell of their hearts
> To eat dusty bread.
>
> They do not see cattle cropping red winter grass,
> They do not hear
> Snow water going down under culverts
> Shallow and clear.
>
> They wait, when they should turn to journeys,
> They stiffen, when they should bend.
> They use against themselves that benevolence
> To which no man is friend.
>
> They cannot think of so many crops to a field
> Or of clean wood cleft by an axe.
> Their love is an eager meaninglessness
> Too tense, or too lax.
>
> They hear in every whisper that speaks to them
> A shout and a cry.
> As like as not, when they take life over their door-sills
> They should let it go by.
>
> (19)

We need to understand that Bogan at once includes and excludes herself
from this indictment. "Women," published in her first book, when she was
twenty-six years old, reflects her famous ambivalence about women in general
and thus about her own gender. Mary de Shazer and Cheryl Walker think the
change in syntax in the final couplet ("As like as not . . .") reflects a sympathy
for women and an understanding of our position in the world; Louise Bogan
herself set special store by the poem early in her career since she had it

reprinted for private distribution in 1929. Years later, in a reading of the poem at the Library of Congress, she said that over the years she had learned to appreciate, admire, and value women.[3] It is this complexity of ambivalence that we find registered in Bogan's oeuvre. In fact, "Women" deserves to be read, not as an isolated poem in an anthology, but in the context of a lifelong quest for expression. Louise Bogan is at times contemptuous of women, and herself; at times appreciative of us, and capable of self-love. What one can always expect from her is an art that is as brutally honest as it is perfectionist. At the heart of her work and life is a terrible balance—that precarious tight-rope position between the female and male traditions of poetry, between psychic health that made creativity possible and breakdown that ended it, between love that nourished and love that destroyed. "It is no small thing to know, as precisely as Louise Bogan did, what it is to be a woman," wrote Ruth Limmer in her introduction to the letters (WWL viii). In the end, if closely read, the poetry that seems to conceal in fact reveals worlds—probably much more than even Louise Bogan knew. The major purpose of this book is to send readers to her poetry. For us, her work is valuable in itself, and a crucial piece of that puzzle we are working on, the puzzle of the female poetic tradition.

Part I

Negotiating between the Traditions

I.

OUTLINES OF AN ARTIST'S LIFE

L'accent et le caractère du pays où l'on est
né demeure dans l'esprit et dans le coeur
comme dans le langage. (The accent and
character of one's native region live in the
mind and heart just as in one's speech.)

—La Rochefoucauld

Louise Marie Bogan was born in 1897 in Livermore Falls, Maine, into a white-collar Irish Catholic family. Her early years were marked by the quarrels of her parents and the absence of her mother. Bogan's memories of childhood are evoked in her journals—the most directly personal writing she ever released. These memoirs were written during her fifties and sixties and published posthumously in the *New Yorker* in 1978 and then in *Journey Around My Room* in 1980. In the memoirs, Bogan is interested in those incidents of childhood that stand out in memory, the remembrances that seem abstracted from, lifted beyond, the reality of all that surrounds them. These events are important precisely because they are the ones that as children we choose to remember; it is these memories that we carry into adult life, these memories that mark us. Thus, as Bogan designed them, the journals evoke the feeling for her of growing up, even though they may not be precisely accurate in every detail. (For example, the journals give the impression of a poverty-stricken youth: in fact, the "poverty" was more spiritual than material.) This was her idea of memoir: "And I think the only thing to do, in these dead areas, is to put down something one has noticed, and not experienced actually. A bird's-eye or a mouse's-eye view. Told with the most careful details and feeling for truth. Then the truth will be bearable, because the truth always comes out queer."[1]

The language of the journals is haunting: Bogan evokes a merciless Maine landscape; frequent moves; a mother who was sometimes depressed, sometimes gay, who would suddenly dress up to go out, who would disappear for long periods; a father, in the shadows, longing for his wife but without the strength to hold her. The setting is

[t]he incredibly ugly mill towns of my childhood, barely dissociated from the empty, haphazardly cultivated, half wild, half deserted countryside around them. Rough stony pastures, rugged woodlots, lit up and darkened by the clearly defined, pale lonely light. . . . (JAR 23)

This is the landscape of her first volume of poems, *Body of This Death* (1923), "a land with hills like rocky gates / Where no sea leaps upon itself" ("A Tale," BE 3). Emptiness reigns in these early poems, with its imagery of unpeopled landscapes.

It is hardest for her to write about her mother. "People lived in intense worlds beyond me" (JAR 23). This single sentence is one paragraph. We have that full stop and then

> So that I do not at first see my mother. I see her clearly much later than I smell and feel her—long after I see those solid fractions of the houses and fields. She comes in frightfully clearly, all at once. . . . (JAR 23)

This is the careful pacing of the journals; passages rise to a crescendo, an emotional crisis, and then are let down, sometimes suddenly, sometimes slowly. The impression left by the whole is one of a recovery of memory through many sessions with an analyst, or a nightmare.

> But one (and final) scene of violence comes through. It is in lamplight, with strong shadows, and an open trunk is in the center of it. The curved lid of the trunk is thrown back, and my mother is bending over the trunk, and packing things into it. She is crying and she screams. My father, somewhere in the shadows, groans as though he has been hurt. It is a scene of the utmost terror. And then my mother sweeps me into her arms, and carries me out of the room. . . . (JAR 26)

This is a dramatization achieved by artistry, of course; but how vivid are the childhood memories from which it is made. Resolution comes with: "I never truly feared her. Her tenderness was the other side of terror" (JAR 27). This ambivalent relationship with her mother, this experience of loss and betrayal is one of the central themes of her poetry. On the one hand, her mother left her. On the other, "all my talent comes from my mother's side" (4 Mar. 1941, 34, n2).

Children bred in chaos long for order. The Bogans once boarded with a family whose life was a model of calm:

> But with the Gardners it was different. Order ran through the house. There were no bare spaces, or improvised nooks and corners; the kitchen shone with paint and oilcloth; the parlor, though miniscule, was a parlor through and through. The dining room, with its round table always ready for a meal (the turning castor-set in the center, the white damask cloth) was used to eat in, three times a day, and the meals were always on time. . . . (JAR 13)

At the Gardners, the young girl saw design and pattern, in the arrangement of flowers, of rooms. She needed this beauty and order, and she would reproduce it in her poems and prose. This is her description of a hospital visit to see her mother:

> Here is what I saw. Someone had put, rather casually, certainly, into a small glass vase, a bunch of what I now know is a rather common garden flower called French marigold. The flowers were dark yellow, with blotches and speckles of brown, and they had, I think, a few rather carrot-like leaves mixed with them. The sight of these flowers gave me such a shock that I lost sight of the room for a moment. . . . Suddenly I *recognized* something at once simple and full of the utmost richness of design and contrast that was mine. A whole world, in a moment, opened up. . . . (JAR 22)

Bogan was forever grateful that her mother arranged for her to attend the Girls' Latin School after the family moved to Boston in 1909. Here Bogan found lessons, and teachers, who nurtured her gift. The drawing instructor was especially crucial: ". . . Miss Cooper, stamped all over with the color and designs of art as well as by the traits of gentility, made double claim upon my respect and imagination" (JAR 40). Bogan wrote her first poems in these years and they were published in the school's literary magazine. It was a significant apprenticeship.

> I went to the Girls' Latin School in the autumn of 1910, at the age of thirteen, for five most fruitful years. I began to write verse from about fourteen on. The life-saving process then began. By the age of 18 I had a thick pile of manuscript, in a drawer in the dining room—and had learned every essential of my trade. (JAR 50)

Bogan, then, had a sense of her vocation very early. She read the Romantics and Pre-Raphaelites as a teenager; this was an influence she felt she had to exorcise later in order to become a mature poet. She went on to study at Boston University but stayed for only a year. Academic training was never for her. Besides, she wanted to get away from home and especially from her mother. And like most girls her age, she had great expectations for romance. In 1916, nineteen years old, in love and wanting to express sexual passion, she turned down a scholarship to Radcliffe and married. Her husband was an army officer; they lived in the East for a time and then moved to the Panama Canal Zone, where he was stationed. A year later, Bogan had a daughter, Maidie. The marriage was troubled from the start; Bogan would say later: "All we had in common was sex. Nothing to talk about. We played *cards*" (JAR xxii).

In 1919 Bogan left her husband; in 1920 he died of pneumonia. Some of the early, never re-published poems, as well as those of *Body of This Death*, register the painful disappointment of this youthful period. Years later, with courage and characteristic good humor, Bogan summed up that time:

> I was the highly charged and neurotically inclined product of an extraordinary childhood and an unfortunate early marriage, into which last state I had rushed to escape the first. I had no relations whatever with the world about me; I lived in a dream, populated by figures out of Maeterlinck and Pater and Arthur

Symons and Compton Mackenzie (*Sinister Street* and *Sylvia Scarlett* made a great impression on me) and H. G. Wells and Francis Thompson and Alice Meynell and Swinburne and John Masefield and other oddly assorted authors. What I did and what I felt was, I assure you, *sui generis*. (11 June 1937, n6)

Bogan claims to have been utterly original in her attitudes. Perhaps she was. Most young girls do not read Maeterlinck and Symons; our romantic fantasies are stirred by more common materials. Yet one effect of youthful reading was the same for Bogan as for many young girls—an utterly unrealistic attitude toward love that is changed only by experience. For Bogan, the dose of reality was: marriage, a child, a separation, and widowhood, all between the ages of nineteen and twenty-two. In 1920 she was living alone in New York City. Her mother and father took Maidie, and Louise visited them on occasional weekends. She took odd jobs, at libraries and bookstores, wrote poems, and had a love affair. In 1923, when she was twenty-six, her first book was published. She dedicated *Body of This Death* to her mother and daughter.

Bogan, young, energetic and attractive, began to make literary friends in New York. Rolphe Humphries and Edmund Wilson, some of her earliest acquaintances, would remain friends for life. Pictures from the period show a woman tall and proud, with great grey eyes. In 1923, Bogan met Raymond Holden and fell in love. She was twenty-six and still hopeful of mature passion. Holden was independently wealthy, a poet and novelist, a "womanizer," some say, an "amiable mediocrity," according to Edmund Wilson.[2] Yet he was a man who was deeply attracted to this difficult young woman poet. Bogan and Holden lived together for a time and then married, setting up housekeeping in New York City and then Santa Fe, New Mexico, and finally in upstate New York. Maidie came to live with them; this was the first "father" she had known. Letters from the early days of marriage are full of news of literary parties and bubbly domestic talk: "We have taken a little apartment with a big sunny *kitchen*—you see, I did get one after all. It's going to be extremely jolly, and I must admit that domesticity thrills me to the bone. Yesterday I made peach jam!" (25 Aug. 1924, 22). Relative happiness prevailed for almost four years. Bogan was able to work. In 1929 she published her second book, *Dark Summer,* whose setting is the farmland country where the Holdens had bought a house. Then things started falling apart. In 1929, "the day after Christmas, while we were away on a visit, our house in the country took fire through the carelessness of the man who was tending the furnace, and burned completely" (6 Jan. 1930, 55). The Holdens had completely redone and refurbished the old farmhouse. They lost their furniture and books and pictures. Bogan lost all her journals, her poems in progress—her work. Always proud and courageous, she told friends not to think her a tragic figure. But the loss to a writer of her work is incalculable.

Around the same time, troubles in her marriage surfaced. Because of her early experiences with her mother, Bogan expected betrayal in relationships. (It is this betrayal theme in *Dark Summer* to which we will give detailed attention in a later chapter.) Unfortunately, Raymond Holden fulfilled his wife's expectations all too well: Their neuroses were a perfect fit. In 1931 the pressures of love and work became too much for the poet and she suffered her first "nervous breakdown." She was back home only two months later, aware that she was "better, although by no means completely well" (23 June 1931, 59). Bogan was grappling with her illusions about romantic love and the relationship of work to her life. Her marriage with Holden was coming to a slow, unbearable end. She had to end it in order to continue her work as poet. She tried to get away by taking a Guggenheim year in Europe but stayed only five months. When she came back, Holden had another woman living in their apartment.

Bogan's journal from September 1933 is a direct expression of the horror of the relationship; through the journals, she was trying to figure out why she stayed. She tried to come to terms with Holden: "the adolescent image he has of himself: the passionate lover, the poet drowned in his lover's arms." But she could not break loose, for "I am not yet ready to stand by myself . . ." (JAR 76). The relationship let her play out her childhood experience of maternal love and betrayal: "The situation could not fit the needs of my own obsessions better if it had been planned for them [to complete them] by some fiendish omniscient being. The distrust, the insecurity I feel shatters me open like repeated blows, and yet, at the present, I can do nothing. I am unable to *will* anything, in order to get away" (JAR 76). Facing up to these realities brought on a second "nervous breakdown." This time Bogan stayed in treatment six months. When she came back to New York in 1934, at the age of thirty-seven, she split up with Holden for good.[3] The thought of sustaining work helped to pull her through the crisis. Edmund Wilson's letters were also an important source of support. At the end of 1933, for example, he wrote to her at the sanitarium and encouraged her to keep working: "What you really ought to do . . . is to give literary expression to your internal conflicts and ranklings. . . . Once you get experience out of your system in a satisfactory literary form, you can thumb your nose at the world. In any case, get out of there as soon as you can—the world needs you, and you, it."[4]

A little less than two years after her second breakdown (and following an eviction from her New York apartment because she could not pay the rent, Holden having reneged on his support payments), Bogan was able to write:

> I am happy now—happy for the first time in my life. At peace for the first time. . . . I'm just going to try to keep that way, that is all. I know it takes work. I worked and fought for thirty-seven years, to gain serenity at thirty-eight. Now I have it. And it's not dependent upon the whim of any fallible human creature, or upon economic security or the weather. I don't know where it comes from. Jung states that such serenity is always a miracle, and I think the saints said that, too. Though there are certain ways, and a certain road that may bring it about, when it comes, it is always a miracle. I am so glad that the therapists of my maturity and the saints of my childhood agree on one score. (7 Oct. 1935, 109)

Bogan's serenities never lasted forever, and so any moment of peace felt like a miracle. In 1935 she had begun an affair with Theodore Roethke. As divorce proceedings started in 1936, she wrote to him of her recent visit with an old friend: "I saw Léonie Adams and her husband recently, and I was more than ever convinced that a spinster's life is to be the future for me." Bogan had been forced to give up many illusions and this was one of them: "Wifehood is too damned full of hero-husband-worship for one of my age and disabusedness" (19 Feb. 1936, 126). She now lived alone—but was not alone. She defended her new way of life to a friend: "Aloneness is peculiar-making, to some extent, but not any more so . . . than lots of Togetherness I've seen" (To Morton D. Zabel, 29 July 1939, 192–93).

In 1937, after her mother's death, Bogan decided to go to Ireland. William Maxwell tells us that this trip created great anxiety. ("The faces in Dublin were, she wrote to her daughter, the faces of conspirators. She grew frightened.")[5] She met a man who helped her; she explained to her friend Morton Zabel:

> There must be a God, Morton, for on the Southampton boat-train, there appeared a tall thin man who proceeded to take care of me like a baby. (No, Morton: it's not another of those things. This was probably, is,—the Angel Gabriel in disguise!) . . . He says *Nuttin* when he means *Nothing;* his parents came from Sligo . . . I told him the whole story [presumably of her panic and its reasons] the second day out, and he nursed me along even more tenderly, thereafter. He laughed me out of it; he tricked me into deck chairs; he brought me lots of rye when the panic became too bad. But for that touch of human understanding, I should certainly have started gibbering.[6]

This was the relationship that would last eight years although, predictably, Bogan tried to destroy it. At one point she sent her new lover a *postcard* breaking things off and he called her back on the phone, "yelling 'What in hell *is* this!' "[7] Bogan felt the conflict between what she had become and where she had come from; in this case, she was more comfortable with a man from her own class background. She would write to Theodore Roethke after this incident: "O, why didn't I know about the trades, years ago? I wasted a lot of time on the professions."[8] For Bogan, this was the only non-obsessive heterosexual relationship of her life. She described it to May Sarton years later:

> During my illness, all this [her obsessive manner of loving] had to be relinquished, step by step. A new personality (that had been coming into light and growth) slowly emerged; and it is this person that you now know. The successful love-affair which began when I was 39 and lasted for 8 years was utterly different from anything that had gone before; perfect freedom, perfect detachment, no *jealousy* at all—an emphasis on *joy,* that is. This is the only kind of relationship that is possible for me now; something *given by me* and received in an almost childish way. (28 Jan. 1954, 282–83)

Through all of this—the attacks of anxiety and breakdowns, the coming to terms with obsessive love—she kept writing, if not poems, letters or journal entries or articles. Bogan's collected papers at the library at Amherst University leave one with the overwhelming impression that she was *always* working—always writing, or thinking about writing, or reading in preparation to write. In 1931, to make a steady living, she had become poetry critic for the *New Yorker*. She could not have known that she would stay on for thirty-eight years nor could she have anticipated the cost. The books never stopped coming. She had to work on a prose style for which she had no large gift. These were hours taken away from poetic quest. She labored over these critical pieces and sometimes it shows: To read *The Poet's Alphabet* now, that collection of her critical judgments, is to be impressed by the generosity and accuracy of her taste but to find the prose a little stuffy, and *weighted*. "One need only imagine," wrote May Sarton with deep understanding, "what it must be to have every book of poems published pile up week by week to realize that such a weight stifles any impulse of one's own. It must feel like being buried under rubble."[9] Yet work on the *New Yorker* also brought Bogan into The Poetry World as one of the arbiters of taste. She claimed not to play literary politics, remaining true to her sense of what was right—though she could be as opinionated as anyone.

Nineteen thirty-seven was indeed a landmark year. It was the year she began her new love affair and celebrated her fortieth birthday, greeted with joy by reading Yeats. ("This morning I arose, bathed, made a superb cup of coffee and two pieces of superior toast, ate these, after eating a fine summer pear. Then I took down Yeats, saying to myself: 'You'd better begin your forty-first year with a little poetry, my girl' " [11 Aug. 1937, 160]). In 1937, too, her third book of poems, *The Sleeping Fury,* was published, dedicated to Edmund Wilson, who had been a good and sustaining friend during the painful years of her breakdowns and the end of her marriage. Bogan's letters in the late thirties register a great buoyancy: "After all, the worst has happened" (9 Oct. 1937, 165).

In 1939 her editor talked her into doing a volume of collected poems. *Poems and New Poems* was published in 1941. Never a fast writer and ever the perfectionist, Bogan was having a hard time calling up her lyric gift. The book had fourteen new poems, including some *Ding-Gedichte,* or object poems, drawing upon Rilke's techniques but with the feel of occasional, made-to-order poems. Nonetheless, *Poems and New Poems* also includes some remarkable examples of continued inspiration. "To Be Sung on the Water" is one of Bogan's most melodious songs, "Zone" one of her strongest and calmest (if not resigned) renditions of a coming to maturity. As she approached fifty, she found that the inspiration and energy for poems came less often and she was impatient with this lack of creativity. She wrote to her old friend, Rolphe Humphries:

> . . . I can't seem to be able to self-start, as I once did . . . O dangerous age of 49!
> O thoughts like dahlias and all late, coarse summer flowers, that linger on till

frost. "Emotionally mature," indeed. If I could only write poetry, all would be well . . . Or fall in love with gusto, in a coarse, dahlia-like way! . . . No creative work in five years! . . . "No wonder you are calm," as you said to me once, ". . . the daemon has been silenced, and whatever silenced it is sitting pretty." (7 Oct. 1946, 254–55)

Bogan linked love and poetry, and much of her work was inspired by passion and its disappointments. She felt pessimistic about the possibilities for love in the later years, writing in 1960 of "the great kindling power of passionate love, which in age we either do not have or do not allow ourselves to feel . . . with women the inhibition is particularly strong: there are so many ways in which they can make fools of themselves . . ." (JAR 167). She needed calm to stay sane but too much calm meant no upwellings of poetry. It was a delicate balance. There is some fulfillment of her own prophecies here; she did not really *expect* either to love or to be able to write in her later years. She was grateful that Humphries gave her some help in 1949 with "Song for the Last Act" (inspired by her meeting with Eliot), "so at least one more poetic work will be published proving that *women* can carry on to some slight degree, in their 50's" (Jan. 1949, 267, n1). Between 1941 and 1954, Bogan published only three poems—"Song for the Last Act," "Train Tune," and "After the Persian."

Yet Bogan was not idle; in her later years, she finally began to receive some of the recognition she deserved. In the forties, she was invited for university teaching stints, sat on fellowship boards and in 1945 was appointed as a consultant in poetry to the Library of Congress. In fact, she was very busy. In the fall of 1948, this is what she had going: "Well, things are narrowing down somewhat. Only a MS to be read (at a $15 fee for Macmillan), a talk to be written ("On the Pleasures of Formal Verse"), to be given at Bard, in *opposition* to W. C. Williams . . . and plans to be made for clothes, etc., for the Fellows' Meeting at the L. of C.—a meeting moved into this November . . . because of T. S. Eliot's presence . . . So I shall at last behold Him in the flesh: yellow eyes and all!" (24 Oct. 1948, 263). There were plenty of writing jobs. She was doing more and more translations. Criticism also took a great deal of energy. She was still writing reviews for the *New Yorker* and in 1951 she published *Achievement in American Poetry, 1900–1950*. That same year she began to gather the pieces for *Selected Criticism* (1955). Her busy literary life continued. She travelled to Europe and to the West Coast and then to Ohio to receive an honorary doctorate. She collaborated on *A Cookbook for Poor Poets and Others* and went to movies and saw Martha Graham dance and read everything and wrote letters and read manuscripts for the Guggenheims. She was often lonely. She became mentor and friend to a younger woman writer, May Sarton, and lived through the death of some of her best friends, including Morton Zabel and Theodore Roethke. She tried hard to accept the changes in her life, to find replacements for love and poetry.

In 1964 Bogan went to Brandeis as a visiting professor. The return to Boston and the scenes of her childhood sent her into a depression:

This depressed state began . . . with the return to the scenes of my childhood—
or adolescence. Boston is really filled with sorrowful memories of my family and
my early self.—I thought, because I had "insight" into it all, that I could rise
above it. But H. has told me that a depression can *seep through,* as it were, in any
case. . . . (12 June 1965, 362)

In June of 1965 she went to the Neurological Institute in New York. The
doctors prescribed Librium, which came on the market in the early sixties and
was promoted as an effective cure for alcoholism.[10] It has been described as a
"minor tranquilizer used to relieve anxiety, tension, and the withdrawal symp-
toms of acute alcoholism." Commonly prescribed for women, its overuse
can "produce somnolence, confusion, diminished reflexes, coma, possibly
death."[11] Bogan immediately began feeling side-effects she associated with the
drugs—heart palpitations and tears—and she had "the semi-knowledge that
the doctor was just as much at sea as you were. (This was nonsense, of course,
as H. is tops in his field.) . . . One evening, with a gibbous moon hanging over
the city (such *visions* we have!) like a piece of red cantaloupe . . . I thought I
had reached the edge of eternity, and *wept* and *wept*" (26 June 1965, 363).
Such visions are typical for users of Librium. One woman interviewed by the
authors of *The Tranquilizing of America* reported her "wonderful feeling" an
hour after taking ten milligrams of Librium: "I thought that the world around
me had turned all warm and mellow. Colors became softer and more diffuse. I
felt like I had been wrapped up in a wonderfully protective coating of foam
rubber that insulated me from the dirt, the grime, the madness, and the noise of
New York."[12] Elizabeth Frank confirms our sense that Bogan was getting
medication in too large doses.[13] In September of 1965 Bogan was transferred
to the hospital in White Plains where she had been thirty years before. She
blamed herself for her condition, writing in apology to Ruth Limmer, "I have
neglected you—and many far-flung friends—in the course of the development
of my 'mind shock' experiences. First off, I was *demoted* from the 'class' I
entered this hospital in; secondly, the days pass in a strangely disjointed
manner" (26 Sept. 1965, 364). Elizabeth Roget is convinced that the electric
shock treatments permanently altered Bogan's capacity to think and create; it
is well known that memory loss is one of the inevitable outcomes of
electroshock.[14] Because she insisted on taking responsibility for everything,
Bogan blamed herself for the effects both of the Librium and the shock
treatments. She continued to take Librium after four months in the hospital.
The pills provided temporary relief and then brought her down, producing fits
of weeping. In August of 1965 she wrote, "I am not taking 2 pills in the
A.M.—one at 7:30 and one around 10:30.—This morning I thought the 1st
pill was going to see me through; a clear, untroubled interval would show up
(take over) every so often . . . But soon that secondary sort of *yearning hunger*
(which is not real hunger, but is in someway attached to the drug) began again.
Heart bumps also slightly involved." She took herself to task for her inability
to pull herself together: "A deep-seated masochism? Surely I have acted in a

consistently *optimistic* fashion, ever since the 1933 breakdown.—I have sur-
mounted one difficulty after another; I have *worked* for life and "creativity"; I
have cast off all the anxieties and fears I could; I have helped others to work
and hold on. Why this collapse of psychic energy . . . why can't I refuel—
recover?" (JAR 174–75). A year later, in July 1966, she was fighting the
torrent of tears which were now Librium's side-effect: "My strange little (for it
must be a child-ghost, embedded in the subconscious) morning visitant is, I
believe, yielding to work-exorcism, more than to medication. *It* vanished at
10:30 a.m. today, and hasn't been back. Work at the typewriter seems to bore
it. For all it wants to do is *weep*. O heavens, am I seeing the end of the tunnel,
at last?" (25 July 1966, 369). "Little Lobelia's Song" (BE 132) registers the
sense that all the old neuroses were coming back to haunt her, once again; and
in it, too, sounds the fear of death. Bogan wrote "Little Lobelia" and "Psychiatrist's Song" in the winter of 1966–67. In 1967, remarkably, she went to
England and Scotland for pleasure. Never one to complain, she acknowledged
in 1968 that she felt cut off: "I get pretty lonely. This is a new feeling, for I
have always been pretty vigorous and self-sufficient. A slight failure of nerve,
no doubt. . . . But I hate it, and wish it would go away" (18 May 1968, 374).
In 1969 she was elected to the American Academy of Arts and Letters. In
that year her last collection was published. Few seemed to notice the appearance of *The Blue Estuaries, Poems 1923–1968*. "My poems seem to have
fallen down that deep, dark well. Not a review! This doesn't bother me
much," she wrote to Ruth Limmer (26 March 1969, 378). But *of course* it
bothered her.

The "side" effects of the Librium, and the lasting effect of the shock
treatments, made it impossible to continue the *New Yorker* poetry reviews. She
gathered up her courage and quit in October 1969. "After 38 years . . . I've had
it. No more pronouncements on lousy verse. No more *hidden* competition. No
more struggling *not* to be a square" (1 Oct. 1969, 381). Immediately after, she
felt much better. "I have exorcised the demon. I'm free. No more A.M. weeping.
No more *fear. The books* go back to the magazine tomorrow . . ." (9 Oct.
1969, 382). But then the emptiness came flowing in. Always a lover of drink,
she had prided herself on the ability to control it. This control was necessary,
especially in her later years, when she became diabetic. Moreover, with the
prescription of Librium, doctors said she must not have more than two drinks
a day.

On 4 February 1970 Elizabeth Roget went to visit Louise Bogan as they had
planned. When there was no answer at the door, Roget went in (she had a key)
with "her heart in her mouth" because she was worried that Bogan had been
drinking too much.[15] She found Bogan dead. May Sarton has pointed out that
there was no autopsy although "coronary occlusion" is written on the death
certificate.[16] Since so many of our revered women writers have committed
suicide, it is important to underline the fact that Bogan did not. Her life at the
end was exceedingly difficult: Drink and loneliness and psychiatric solutions
did not help. But Louise Bogan was first and foremost a survivor.

What Louise Bogan had faced and *gotten through* was a troubled childhood and the challenge of being woman and poet in the modernist period and the expectations for love and romance and the care of a child and the drain of critical work and drug therapy and a lack of recognition, especially at the end of her life. In the following chapters, we will pursue in detail Bogan's achievements as an artist; our point of departure will be her achievement of a negotiation between the female and male traditions of poetry.

II.

THE AUTHORITY OF MALE TRADITION

[T]he historical sense compels a man to
write not merely with his own generation in
his bones, but with a feeling that the whole
of the literature of Europe from Homer and
within it the whole of the literature of his
own country has a simultaneous existence
and composes a simultaneous order.

—T. S. Eliot, "Tradition and
the Individual Talent"

May a poet write as a poet or must he
write as a period?

—Laura Riding and Robert Graves,
A Survey of Modernist Poetry

I have been thinking about Censors. How
visionary figures admonish us . . .

—Virginia Woolf, *Diary*

[T]hose women artists esteemed by men are
not ones to declaim themselves women.
Neither in puzzlement or pain (like Lowell)
nor in bitterness (like Louise Bogan).

—Florence Howe, *No More Masks!*

To think about literary influence in the case of a woman writer is to find
oneself in the midst of a special complexity. The woman writer must contend
with two traditions: that tradition which has been considered normative,
universal—the male literary tradition—and that writing which until recently
was not thought of in terms of a tradition but as a kind of minor current
flowing below the mainstream—the writing of women. The work of Louise
Bogan gives us a particularly compelling opportunity to see how these two

traditions conjoin in the poetry and thought of a distinguished woman of letters writing from the twenties through the forties in America. It is clear, on the one hand, that the woman poet comes to the tradition of male poetry from a different route than men; and it is also clear that in one way or another she must contend both with the women writers who preceded her and those who are writing in her own time. Some women poets do not make a point of avoiding the label "woman poet"; Louise Bogan, however, began her career by publicly dissociating herself from other female poets. She made it quite clear she wanted to be placed among the poets of the mainstream (male) tradition. In 1939 Bogan agreed to respond to a *Partisan Review* questionnaire on literary influence. She had in the past declined such requests, being private both about her life and her influences. By 1939, however, she was more conscious about her image as a poet: She had published three major books and was well ensconced as the *New Yorker*'s poetry editor. The *Partisan Review* asked if she was "conscious, in your own writing, of the existence of a 'usable past,' " if that usable past was primarily American, and to what extent she thought Whitman and James were crucial to the development of an American literary tradition.[1] It is clear from her response that Louise Bogan's idea of what poetry should be came from that canon of male poets taught in literature courses in high school and college. Her response shows she wanted to be seen in terms of that tradition. She pointed first to her classical background:

> Because what education I received came from New England schools, before 1916, my usable past has more of a classic basis than it would have today, even in the same background. The courses in English literature which I encountered during my secondary education and one year of college were very nutritious. But my "classical" education was severe, and I read Latin prose and poetry and Xenophon and the *Iliad* during my adolescence.[2]

From this early study of the Latin poets Bogan first experienced the pleasures of formal poetry, pleasures of rhythm and control that would remain at the center of her aesthetic. Rhythm for her was bound up with human life: "So we see man, long before he has much of a 'mind,' celebrating and extending and enjoying the rhythms of his heartbeat and of his breath." And: "We think of certain tasks the rhythm of which has become set. Sowing, reaping, threshing, washing clothes . . ." (PA 152).

In her response to the *Partisan Review,* Bogan went on to acknowledge the modernist poets and their predecessors who in the late nineteenth and early twentieth century changed ideas of what poetry should be. It is not surprising that Bogan, who was always acutely aware of literary currents and was a self-educated literary historian, looked to these poets:

> Arthur Symons' *The Symbolist Movement,* and the French poets read at its suggestion, were strong influences experienced before I was twenty. The English metaphysicals (disinterred after 1912 and a literary fashion during my twenties) provided another literary pattern, and Yeats influenced my writing from 1916,

when I first read *Responsibilities*. The American writers to whom I return are Poe (the *Tales*), Thoreau, E. Dickinson and Henry James. Whitman, read at sixteen, with much enthusiasm, I do not return to.[3]

Thus, Bogan's strategy is to invoke the dominant tradition and to place herself within it. I want now to focus on the center of her response, the attribution of influence to the symbolists, the metaphysicals and Yeats, for here are the roots and the flower of modernism, that tradition in which Louise Bogan wanted her own work to find its place. I will save discussion of the only American, and the only woman in this list, Emily Dickinson, for the next chapter, and will remark upon those influences, such as Rilke, who are not mentioned in this catalogue. What Bogan leaves out of this official list is as interesting as what is put in; the list shows us her idea of the way she wished to be seen in terms of the history of poetry.

Thus, before we proceed, I want to add the complication of gender to this list of influences. Only time and distance would make it possible for Bogan to speak directly on this subject. The issues she raises in the following passage from her *Achievement in American Poetry, 1900–1950,* published in 1951, were barely under the surface as she began her literary career. As she opens her chronicle of the development of modern American poetry—after she had nearly completed her contribution to that development—Bogan puts forward the view that Edwin Arlington Robinson had restored some truth to poetry: His contribution was to bring it "from the sentimentality of the nineties toward modern veracity and psychological truth" (AA 20). Yet, according to Bogan, he "did little to reconstitute any revivifying warmth of feeling in the poetry of his time" (AA 22). In her chapter called "The Line of Truth and the Line of Feeling," Bogan then goes on to point out who did bring that "warmth of feeling" to poetry:

> This task, it is now evident, was accomplished almost entirely by women poets through methods which proved to be as strong as they seemed to be delicate. The whole involved question of woman as artist cannot be dealt with here. We can at this point only follow the facts, as they unfold from the later years of the nineteenth century to the beginning of the twentieth: these facts prove that the line of poetic intensity which wavers and fades out and often completely fails in poetry written by men, on the feminine side moves on unbroken. Women, as "intuitive" beings, are less open to the success and failures, the doubts and despair which attack reason's mechanisms. Women's feeling, at best, is closely attached to the organic heart of life. . . . (AA 22-23)

Bogan assiduously avoids "the question of the woman artist" (although in her later years she liked to quote Henry James's line about "that oddest of animals, the artist who happens to be born a woman" [JAR 136]). She brings together those seeming opposites, strength and delicacy, as the special characteristics of women such as Lizette Woodworth Reese and Louise Imogen Guiney. Although she did not speak openly about it until the fifties, this idea of woman's gift would have a profound impact on Bogan's assessment of what was valuable in poetry and what she could use from the dominant tradition. As we look more closely at Bogan's public statement for the *Partisan Review*, let us keep in mind the limitations and problems inherent in any study of influence. For the sake of this study, I define as "influences" those poets from whom Bogan learned the lessons of craft and whose examples gave or denied her permission to express certain kinds of emotion in poetry. The earliest influences were the most crucial ones, those that carried her through her relatively brief lyric career. Ours will be an excursion into the ways in which Bogan's work differs from, and is similar to, those artists she invokes as a literary pattern; for, as we shall see, the male tradition has limited usefulness for the woman poet. It is, in fact, my contention that Bogan absorbed the stylistic lessons of modernism and then used those techniques to elaborate a necessarily different subject matter, the themes of love, madness, and art derived from her life as an American woman. Moreover, as our final chapters will show, although she learned from and used the male modernist tradition, she paradoxically made a major contribution to the development of a female tradition in poetry. In other words, as she used the male tradition, she transformed it for women.

Louise Bogan's letters and critical work contain many more references to the symbolists and to Yeats than to the metaphysicals. She read the symbolists early in her career and then in 1936 she carefully reread Baudelaire, Mallarmé, and Rimbaud. ("This morning I got down five or six notebooks, that have been gathering dust in the back closet, and discovered how v. studious I was in 1936. Pages and pages in French and English . . ." [To May Sarton, 23 May 1954, 288] Of the three major symbolist poets, I think only Mallarmé had any direct influence on her style, although his subject matter, as we shall see, was not open to her. She identified with Rimbaud's irreverence ("He did the only thing a poet *should* do: he shocked hell out of everyone by a series of semi-criminal acts, and then he got out, for good and all" [To Rolphe Humphries, 26 Sept. 1938, 176]), but she did not think the "surrealist" mode suitable for women. Most of her writing about Baudelaire was occasioned by new translations of his work, including a 1947 version, which prompted her to speak of "the first poet who saw through the overweening pretensions of his time" (PA 52). She also noted that "the working of this stylistic machine are now outmoded. And nothing is more tiresome than the reiterated subject—so usual in the early Baudelaire—of women as puppet, as sinister idol of the alcove, or as erotic mannequin" (PA 51). Bogan's early understanding of what we now call "images of women" in male literature is remarkable—but what interests us most here is that Baudelaire's French rhetoric was too outdated for a modern American poet to use in any direct way. We can only say that Bogan is distantly related to Baudelaire, in the sense of a long historical line that finally produced modern poetry, since the compactness and the intensity of the modernist lyric do owe something to the author of *Les Fleurs du Mal*.

We do not always agree today with its critical judgments but Arthur Symons's *The Symbolist Movement* was important because it introduced the French poets to an English-speaking audience. For Symons, Mallarmé's art of suggestion, the evocation of emotion, the emotion itself in the poem, brought something new to the art:

> "Poetry," said Mallarmé," is the language of a state of crisis"; and all his poems are the evocation of a passing ecstasy, arrested in mid-flight. This ecstasy is never the mere instinctive cry of the heart, the simple human joy or sorrow . . . which he did not admit in poetry. It is a mental transposition of emotion or sensation, veiled with atmosphere, and becoming, as it becomes a poem, pure beauty.[4]

In this dramatic, hyperbolic passage, we have the idea of an emotion caught by the poet, a technique Bogan imitated. Yet for her there was nothing trivial about "the cry of the heart." In fact, she once said that she could not write novels because "my talent is for the cry or the *cahier* . . ." (To Theodore Roethke, 6 Nov. 1935, 117). For Mallarmé, as one contemporary critic has written, "the more rigidly the poetic symbol excludes the world of natural reality and the initial emotion the more closely it approximates the ideal of art."[5] Bogan's poetry depends on this initial emotion: "Lyric poetry, if it is at all authentic . . . is based on emotion—on some real occasion, some real confrontation," she wrote (To Sister M. Angela, 20 Aug. 1966, 368).

From Mallarmé and the modernist school that followed him Bogan learned distancing, surely. Yet it is a matter of degree; she would not move so far from the emotion as to disown it. Although his extreme attitude toward emotion in poetry was not her own, Mallarmé's technique was instructive for her. In 1954 she praised one of May Sarton's poems because it used a symbol like the center of a wheel, with spokes radiating out from, and returning to, the poem's center: "I liked 'Little Fugue,' unbreakable old symbolist that I am: a central symbol holds all together, and yet radiates. . . . This grand (in the Irish sense) method Mallarmé passed on to us. . . ."[6] In order to make this point more concretely—and to show how Bogan carved out a poetic territory influenced by, but different from, that of her male masters—let us look closely at one of the most famous examples of a work that articulates Mallarmé's flight into a pure realm of art.[7] "Les Fenêtres" harks back to Baudelaire and looks forward to the English symbolists. I have selected this poem for its expression of a dominant modernist theme; only later would Mallarmé develop to their fullest the new techniques these themes made necessary. There are many other poems I might have chosen to illustrate the escape into pure beauty—and its concomitant flight from life—that characterizes male poetry from the late nineteenth century through the 1920s; I have selected this one because it stands at the beginning of a poetic tradition upon which Mallarmé had enormous influence. For in "Les Fenêtres" Mallarmé imagines a dying man in a hospital, weary of flesh and material reality, who presses his pale face up against a window bathed in sunlight. There he finds a kind of Baudelairian vision of peace and beauty that provokes an overwhelming sense of disgust with the material world, represented as women and children:

> Ainsi, pris du dégoût de l'homme a l'âme dure
> Vautré dans le bonheur, où ses seuls appétits
> Mangent, et qui s'entête à chercher cette ordure
> Pour l'offrir à la femme allaitant ses petits,
>
> (Thus, seized with a disgust of man whose hard soul
> Wallows in happiness, where only his appetites
> Eat, and who persists in searching for this filth
> In order to offer it to the woman nursing her children,)

The dying man-poet would leap through the windows to flee the real world. Remarkably, he sees himself reborn as an angel:

> Je fuis et je m'accroche à toutes les croisées
> D'où l'on tourne l'épaule à la vie, et, béni,
> Dans leur verre, lavé d'éternelles rosées,
> Que dore le matin chaste de l'Infini
>
> Je me mire et me vois ange! et je meurs, et j'aime
> —Que la vitre soit l'art, soit la mysticité—
> À renaître, portant mon rêve en diadème,
> Au ciel antérieur où fleurit la Beauté!
>
> (I flee and I hang on to all the windows
> From where one turns one's shoulder away from life, and, blessed,
> In their glass, washed by eternal dews,
> Which gild the chaste morning of the Infinite,
>
> I look at myself and I see myself as an angel! and I die and I love
> —Whether the pane be art or whether it be mysticism—
> To be reborn, wearing my dream like a diadem,
> To the prior heaven where Beauty flowers!)

This would-be angel must be thrust out of reverie and returned to earth: "Mais, hélas, Ici-bas est maître" (But alas! the world below is master). Forced to live with human stupidity, still, in the final stanza his bitter self asks once again, beseechingly, whether there is a way out, an escape from this life down below.

"Les Fenêtres" is a youthful poem, marked by the excesses of youth, yet it registers the sentiments of many modernist poems written before and after it. These are the poems dedicated to an aesthetic that would take life out of art. In the years that followed "Les Fenêtres" Mallarmé succeeded more and more in achieving "total annihilation of the 'life' emotion which inspired the poem."[8] Aspects of this aesthetic would reach into twentieth-century modernist poetry. In "Les Fenêtres" Mallarmé expresses a disgust for the physical, and in an act of hubris rare for a woman who writes and impossible to Bogan, he imagines himself escaping the Real, fleeing to a transcendent realm beyond the glass. He can even see himself as Ange. The modernist aesthetic, when it posits an absolute division between art and life, is antithetical to women's realities. First, a woman is usually in no position to choose life or the state of an angel; she must go on "allaitant ses petits," feeding her children, if not literally her children, then responding to the consuming needs of real human beings. (And if she chooses to entrust the care of her daughter to others at certain points in her life, the woman poet like Bogan or H.D. is accused of consummate selfishness.) Love and relationship is at the root of Bogan's poetry; when she cut herself off, as she did sometimes, in exhaustion, she could not write.

The reader of modern poetry, then, who comes to *The Blue Estuaries* expecting the flight from life, the exclamations over the Void that we see in such poems as "Les Fenêtres," will be thrown off guard, even led to say this is not "good" poetry because it is different. The preoccupation with the Void can be traced to Baudelaire's "gouffre" poems; this is the abyss of nothingness that, for Baudelaire, the Catholic moralist, meant confrontation both with a loss of faith and a hanging on to it. The loss becomes complete among many male writers and thinkers later in the nineteenth century, and into the twentieth, which spawned great variations on this theme of the emptiness of life. The final existential attitude, we now understand, was inimical to most women, who as the guardians of life had neither the luxury nor the predilection to think about non-life. We have said that Bogan learned something about distancing from Mallarmé and the twentieth-century modernists but she never took it as far as her male precursors. Put differently, Bogan used modernist examples to rein in her powerful emotions, but she also wanted feeling and human experience in the poem. This use of modernist form distinguishes her both from the male modernists and from the legacy of female poetry that she wished to counter. In "The Cupola" we have both the distancing and the attachment to experience. The speaker enters a dome-shaped room, a setting inspired perhaps by Bogan's Maine birthplace which had "such a cupola and eaves made of gingerbread. . . ."[9] She finds in this upper room a mirror that reflects nature, the outdoors. Trees and the wind appear in this mirroring:

The Cupola

A mirror hangs on the wall of the draughty cupola.
Within the depths of glass mix the oak and the beech leaf,
Once held to the boughs' shape, but now to the shape of the wind.

Someone has hung the mirror here for no reason,
In the shuttered room, an eye for the drifted leaves,
For the oak leaf, the beech, a handsbreath of darkest reflection.

Someone has thought alike of the bough and the wind
And struck their shape to the wall. Each in its season
Spills negligent death throughout the abandoned chamber.

(34)

The poem illustrates what Bogan learned from the modernists about indirect expression; seen in the context of the other poems in this, her most "removed" volume, *Dark Summer* (1929), the setting becomes a metaphor for the human capacity for destruction. In the first stanza, there is the feeling of the room, the presence of the speaker in it, and the moving of trees reflected in a mirror. Human agency, something even a little frightening, enters in the second, for "someone" has placed the mirror in this room, seemingly for no reason. Yet it provides an "eye," even a double vision for anyone coming into this secret, shuttered place; the lovely, inspired phrase, "a handsbreath of darkest reflection," brings the suggestion that this room yields the chance for greater self-knowledge. The poem grows more violent in the third stanza, repeating the idea of human agency: There is no choice now but to see clearly the destruction that wind and bough bring in their wake. Emotional destruction of some kind; this we know both from the poem and the volume in which it appears. The atmosphere of absence in the poem is inspired by symbolist techniques as is the evocation of the effect of emotion rather than the specific emotion itself. "Peindre non la chose, mais l'effet qu'elle produit" (Paint not the thing itself but the effect it produces), wrote Mallarmé as he began his Hérodiade.[10] For Mallarmé, the effect would have increasing importance; he would eventually try to shape poetry that was "about" nothing. For Bogan, the rendering of emotional experience was always paramount. In "The Cupola" she stays with the inner experience. The poem is a way of understanding experience, not an escape from it. For Bogan, then, the distancing technique operates to register tumultuous human emotion, the effects of terrible division and destruction, feelings that could get out of control in the poem (and in her life) without a contained method for expressing them.

Mallarmé's fenêtre/mirror, on the other hand, beckons toward a realm beyond material reality; Bogan's mirror functions to see human emotional experience doubly. Her sense of the interior scene is dominant: this woman poet is not looking out the window (or leaping out of it) to find transcendent reality. Rather, she is very much in the room, a space she has created. Like many women (and not because of nature but due to nurture) Bogan had a strong sense of interiors. This is evident from her journals, her short story "Journey Around My Room," and from her own rooms, described by May Sarton. Here she is speaking of the apartment where Bogan lived from 1937 until her death in 1970:

> I shall not ever forget walking into the apartment at 137 East 168th Street for the first time, after an all-night drive from Washington. I felt a sharp pang of nostalgia as I walked into that civilized human room, filled with the light of a sensitized, bitter, lucid mind. The impact was so great because not since I walked into Jean Dominique's two rooms above the school in Brussels had I felt so much at home in my inner self. In each instance the habitation reflected in a very special way the tone, the hidden music, as it were, of a woman, and a woman living alone, the sense of a deep loam of experience and taste expressed in the

surroundings, the room a shell that reverberated with oceans and tides and waves of the owner's past, the essence of a human life as it had lived itself into certain colors, *objets d'art,* and especially into many books. . . . Louise's word for this atmosphere was 'life-enhancing.'[11]

Sarton's prose is richly evocative of the surroundings Bogan created for her work. Out of a sense of domestic interiors, her own emotional experience, the lessons of the modernists and the "negative" examples of her female precursors, Louise Bogan created a poem like "The Cupola."

To summarize, then: Although there is some Mallarmian symbolist influence in the qualities of her verse, content is another matter entirely. Mallarmé disdained the crowd; Baudelaire described life as a hospital in which each of the sick desired only to change beds. This attitude is called "the horror of life" by Roger L. Williams in his study of nineteenth-century French authors.[12] I do not wish to dismiss the great contribution of the French tradition but rather to delineate its limitations for a poet like Louise Bogan whose subject matter came from the center of emotional experience. Not impervious to a certain measure of horror and disgust with existence, she nonetheless kept confronting this attitude and reconnecting with a more complex view of life.[13] As we shall see in the next chapter, her sense of the female gift was inextricably linked to the "heart" that women bring to poetry. It is finally paradoxical that one who inveighed against the female tradition ultimately came to define women's talent in almost stereotypical ways and would in her later career criticize those women poets who tried out "male" modes of expression. But of course a stereotyping of female qualities and a revolt against "female" tradition go hand in hand.

The phrasing of Louise Bogan's response to the *Partisan Review* inquiry about literary influence gives us a clue about the relative importance to her of the "metaphysical" poets. Her syntax suggests they were not crucial: They were a "fashion," a "literary pattern," wedged between the larger influences, the symbolists and Yeats. It is, in fact, hard to relate Bogan to the tradition of metaphysical poetry in part because she wrote very little about it and because it is difficult to say exactly what is meant by the term. Samuel Johnson first named this seventeenth-century mode in the eighteenth, and T. S. Eliot, in an essay first published in 1921 which Bogan may have read, linked it to modernism in the twentieth. Eliot's essay focuses on the stylistic properties of the metaphysicals and on their capacity for thought. Certainly this model did not function for Bogan in the same way as it did for Eliot, that is, as a way to bring thought into poetry. Her work is more reflective than intellectual and this stance comes out of her own experience. Bogan herself had a rather specific definition of metaphysical. Writing to May Sarton, she noted, "You have a *metaphysical* bent: you desire the universal behind the apparent; you have a passion for the transcendent" (21 Oct. 1961, 333). Bogan's later meditative poetry asserts connections between the human and the natural world, a philosophy that derives from her own experience of change and time. The "sexual realism" of some of the metaphysicals had an appeal for the moderns, says one commentator: "In its earliest manifestations, it was . . . distinguished by revolutionary and highly original attitudes toward sexual love. . . . A new kind of sexual realism, together with an interest in introspective psychological analysis . . . became an element in the metaphysical fashion."[14] Surely the stylistic influence was most felt by Bogan, the "telescoping of images and multiplied associations," "the brief words and sudden contrasts" that Eliot notes in his essay "The Metaphysical Poets," citing Donne's

A bracelet of bright hair about the bone.[15]

Bogan's "To a Dead Lover," published in 1922 and later suppressed, begins

The dark is thrown
Back from the brightness, like hair
Cast over a shoulder.[16]

Jeanne Kammer was one of the first to point out that women poets come to modernism by a very different route from men. She leads us to another distinction between Bogan's choice of subject matter and the province of the male poets she so admired. For Kammer, the tight, controlled poems of male modernists "represent both a dramatization of and a withdrawal from a culture fragmented, disordered, and lacking in central values and vision." Kammer writes that if women's poems reflect fragmentation, this is an "internal division . . . a private experience opposed to the public one of men."[17] Bogan felt that those large questions of the relationship between man and civilization were not her province; only men, in her view, could write about the wasteland. This attitude is another example of her internalization of ideas of woman's role. She seemed to accept the notion that because men are the creators of civilization, because they instigate and fight its wars, they are uniquely qualified to write about this political realm. She made a distinction between the internal world and the external and she felt her subject, even the *genuine* subject, of art was the internal. In the mid-thirties, during the trauma of the Spanish Civil War and the threat of a second large European conflict, Bogan had terrific fights with her male friends about politics. For her, "politics" was the petty, egotistical fight for power among factions, all of them equally ridiculous. Her own lower middle-class origins had something to do with this attitude: The attempt of intellectuals to save the masses was faintly comic to her. Politics was subsumed under something larger, the movements of History, which had a certain inevitability: " '[H]istory' is itself a stream of energy, is 'generous inconsistency'; and . . . those who work with it succeed best when they realize this, as the artist always realizes it. It can't be pawed out of shape; it must be listened to, before being acted upon" (7 Oct. 1940, 211). It is art that nourishes the soul: "I know, and knew, that politics are nothing but sand and gravel: it is art and life that feed us until we die. Everything else is ambition, hysteria or hatred" (To Theodore Roethke, 14 Dec. 1937, 169). She lamented the effect of politics on the poetry of the thirties: "I still think that poetry has something to do with the imagination; I still think it ought to be well-written. I still think it is private feeling, not public speech" (8 July 1938, 173). These attitudes separated her from many of the male poets of her generation as well as from some of the women. H.D., for example, wrote about the effects of war from a female perspective, focusing on its results for personal relationships; her later poetry would dissect patriarchy and male power. H.D. felt as connected to wars of the present and the past, as affected by them, as men. Millay was criticized by Bogan and many others for her political poetry and activism. We are just beginning to learn the extent of the female literary response to the First and Second World War; the more we know, the more Bogan's rejection of this subject matter seems a "female" response and a further example of the limits she set for her work—limits determined in part by her sense of what was possible to a woman poet of her time who wanted immortality through art.[18]

Bogan's conscious confrontations with the tradition forced her to define herself as a poet. She carved out her own subject matter and her own style. Her emotions were so intense that they often threatened to get out of control: she used the modernist aesthetic to provide a form for her strong feelings. "You will remember, I am sure, in dealing with my work, that you are dealing with emotion under high pressure—so that symbols are its only release," she wrote to one interpreter (To Sister M. Angela, 20 Aug. 1966, 368). If modernism was for her a formal strategy for releasing emotion through symbol and compact form, and a way of putting behind her the influences of her early apprentice-ship, such as Morris and Rossetti, it did not lead to the "depersonalization" advocated by Eliot. In the fifties, she located her aesthetic between the "de-personalization" of her era and the new confessional modes. Writing to May Sarton, she pointed out that in poetry, "certainly, 'unadulterated life' must be transposed, although it need not be 'depersonalized.' Otherwise you get 'self-expression' only; and that is only half of art." The distinctions between "transpose," "adulterated," and "depersonalized" are subtle indeed and un-derstandable only within the context of Bogan's interpretation of the "male" and "female" traditions of poetry, which we are studying here, and their relationship to her particular talent. For Bogan, emotion is central to the poem but to no avail without skill: "The other half is technical, as well as emotional, and the most poignant poems are those in which the technique takes up the burden of the feeling instantly; and that presupposes a practiced tech-nique . . ." (To May Sarton, 17 Mar. 1955, 296). Through the poem the poet is unburdened of that weight of emotion. This idea of the burden of emotion is delineated in a short essay called "The Springs of Poetry," which Bogan published in 1923 and which we will consider in chapter 5. The idea is also strikingly similar to one held by Sara Teasdale. This is Teasdale's theory of poetry as she outlined it in 1919:

My theory is that poems are written because of a state of emotional irritation. It may be present for some time before the poet is conscious of what is tormenting him. The emotional irritation springs, probably, from subconscious combinations of partly forgotten thoughts and feelings. Coming together, like electrical currents in a thunderstorm, they produce a poem. . . . The poem is written to free the poet from an emotional burden. Any poem not so written is only a piece of craftmanship.[19]

Teasdale's emphasis is on the emotion; Bogan, a member of the generation after Teasdale, a modernist, underlines the companionship of craft and feeling.

Bogan, then, felt herself walking a fine line between the two traditions, the female and the male. Because it emphasizes the expression of personal feeling and experience, her work did not fit in with Eliot's pronouncements on "objective poetry"—an aesthetic position that, we should note, had a profound impact on an academic establishment that did not notice Bogan's oeuvre. By the fifties, Bogan had some perspective on other, more extreme manifestations of modern objectivity. Her review of *Auroras of Autumn,* for example, again makes her point about life in poetry. "[N]o one," she writes of Wallace Stevens, "can describe the simplicities of the natural world with more direct skill. It is a natural world strangely empty of human beings, however; Stevens' men and women are bloodless symbols." She feels that his "technique overwhelms the poem: . . . [T]here is something theatrical in much of his writing; his emotions seem to be transfixed rather than released and projected, by his extraordinary verbal improvisations . . ." (PA 382). A preoccupation with technique—sometimes a way to escape feeling—prevents the release of emotion into the poem. In this review Bogan laments that many younger poets try to imitate Stevens as though they did not realize that other kinds of modern poetry tap the "transparent, overflowing and spontaneous qualities that Stevens ignores" (PA 383).

Her belief in a poetry based on confrontation with emotional experience would lead her eventually to Rilke. She read him late, in 1935, writing to her editor, "And I've just discovered Rilke. Why did you never tell me about Rilke? My God, the man's wonderful" (To John Hall Wheelock, 1 July 1935, 86). She used his invention of the *Ding-Gedichte* ("thing-poems") to great advantage in her later poems. His example may have influenced the title poem of *The Sleeping Fury,* published in 1937. In that year, she wrote that Rilke was the "rare example of the poet who, 'having learned to give himself to what he trusted,' finally 'learned to give himself to what he feared' " (PA 349). Her collections from *The Sleeping Fury* onward took as epigraph two lines from Rilke:

> Wie ist das klein, womit wir ringen;
> was mit uns ringt, wie is das gross . . .
>
> (How small is that with which we struggle;
> how great that which struggles with us.)[20]

Louise Bogan's lack of attraction to the more life-denying manifestations of modernism would lead her to feel a greater affinity for Yeats than for Eliot or Stevens. In fact, of all the male influences, Yeats was the most decisive in her early formative years, the only poet writing in English to make such an impact. She read his work early, in 1916, when she was only nineteen, thus four years before the publication of her first volume, *Body of This Death* (1923). Her collected criticism, *A Poet's Alphabet* (1970), includes five essays on Yeats; one dating from 1938 is entitled "The Greatest Poet Writing in English Today." The affinity for Yeats came on many levels. His intensity, his lyricism, his song, mirrored her ambitions for poetry. His aesthetic was hers: "a style of speech as simple as the simplest prose, like the cry of the heart. It is not the business of the poet to instruct his age. His business is merely to express himself, whatever that self may be."[21] Singing is a major theme in her work as it is in Yeats; for Bogan, music was almost as essential as breathing. Her writing on rhythm in poetry often relates the rhythm of breath and song. She played the piano and grew up in a "family of singers: my mother and my brother were constantly 'bursting into song.' And I began to study the piano at seven" (To Sister M. Angela, 5 July 1969, 92). Like Yeats, Bogan had to pull herself away from the influences of the Pre-Raphaelites; like his, her poems could be both bitter and proud. Above all, she admired his enduring capacity for trying to understand his experiences and then transmuting them into art. Her attraction was even more profound because of her Irish roots, an identification strengthened by the immigrant's experience of discrimination: "It was borne in upon me, all during my adolescence, that I was a 'mick,' no matter what my other faults or virtues might be."[22] There were enormous differences as well, those that can be attributed both to class and gender. Yeats had an aristocrat's education, first at home and then in private schools. His central political involvements were far from Bogan's experience. Among Bogan's essays on Yeats, her longest focuses on his role in Irish struggles for artistic and political independence; eventually she would express some impatience with the more conservative expressions of his political life. Nor did she, as a woman who internalized social stereotypes of femininity, have such grand poetic ambitions; Yeats "read a special symbolism into all his private acts and relationships," writes M. L. Rosenthal; and, as Edward Engelberg has pointed out in *The Vast Design,* he developed a complex symbolic system to image his thoughts and feelings.[23] Bogan's aesthetic of limitation decreed that such ambitions were not appropriate to female talent. Moreover, she did not think the idea and argument common to prose was appropriate for lyric poetry. One can find echoes of the early Yeats in early Bogan, in the simplicity of passionate language, even in the melancholy tone; yet she would never use symbol in the way Yeats did in his more philosophical works of the late twenties, after he wrote *A Vision.* In "The Cupola," for example, the image of the mirror insinuates itself into the poem; Yeats, on the other hand, brought to the poem an authoritative or dominant image inspired by his personal mythic system. In fact, much of the power of his later poetry derives from this assertion of a single image.

So far we have seen that the male tradition is authoritative enough that Louise Bogan claimed it and then went on to both selectively use and discard aspects of it. Before we bring to an end this journey into the authority of male influence, I wish to suggest yet another source of inspiration that Bogan did not mention in her catalogue of influences: Johann Wolfgang von Goethe. I realize we are now speaking different languages; however, the direct lyricism, the lack of interest in philosophical themes in the early poems, the "romanticism"—these qualities Bogan shared with the German poet. She read him (with the help of a dictionary and translations) early in her career and in 1924, quoting the "Wandrers Nachtlied," she wrote to a friend:

> The stripped, still lyric moves me more, invariably, than any flummery ode ever written—although, of course, Keats and the Romantics were only partly flummery—but
>
> Über allen Gipfeln
> Ist Ruh
>
> gives me such happiness I want to cry.
>
> (To Rolphe Humphries, 24 July 1924, 9)

Goethe had a remarkable gift for spontaneity—his lyrics are among the most inspired, the most direct and unmediated, I have read. ("Über allen Gipfeln," or so the myth goes, was scrawled in a moment of inspiration on the wall of a mountain hut.) This spontaneity stayed with him all his life. Like Bogan, he was often overwhelmed by Eros, although his love poems tend to be happier than hers and his lyric vein lasted much longer. Bogan worked hard on her German so that she could appreciate its poets. In an essay on Goethe published in 1949, she noted, rightly I think, that he is little appreciated by English-speaking readers because the translations are so poor. For what counts in so many of his lyrics is *sound*. Bogan suggested that those who do not read German listen to Hugo Wolf's songs based on Goethe's lyrics:

> Anyone who has listened to the wild longing of the Wolf-Goethe "Kennst du das Land" or to the noble and transcendent beauty of their "Prometheus" and "Ganymed" has experienced the only world it is important to share with any great poet—the world of his intense emotion and his piercing vision. (PA 201)

Late in her life, this strong affinity for Goethe led to translations of several of his prose works, which she worked on with Elizabeth Mayer. *Elective Affinities* came out in 1963 and *The Sorrows of Young Werther* and *Novelle* in 1971.

What Bogan shares with Goethe, then, is at once a devotion to the formal qualities of art and to intense lyricism, that is, poetry inspired by significant emotional experience. Yet both poets felt they had to learn to check their unrestrained emotions; Goethe's early lyrics are overflowing with passion and energy, and in his middle years, he spoke through *Faust* of the necessity to rein in emotions that threatened to engulf him. Yet he managed to sing of love in old age, too, in the eloquent lyrics of the *West-östlicher Divan*. Ultimately, through Goethe, we realize that Bogan's poetry has as much of a Romantic cast as a modern one. Although he does not link her to Goethe, Harold Bloom some years ago recognized this Romantic heritage:

> Louise Bogan is usually categorized as a poet in the metaphysical tradition or meditative mode, following Donne, Emily Dickinson, and older contemporaries like Eliot and Ransom. Yet, like so many modern poets, she is a Romantic in her rhetoric and attitudes. . . . Miss Bogan is purely a lyrical poet, and lacks the support of the personal systems of Blake and Yeats, by which those poets were able more serenely to contemplate division in the psyche. Miss Bogan is neither a personal mythmaker, in the full Romantic tradition, like her near contemporary Hart Crane, nor an ironist in the manner of Tate, to cite another poet of her generation. The honesty and passion of her best work has about it, in consequence, a vulnerable directness.[24]

The last line of this 1958 evaluation echoes Bogan's point of view in her essay on the female poetic gift, "The Heart and the Lyre" (1947), which I shall discuss in the next chapter. Bloom at once underlines Bogan's specialness as he places her within a part of the male tradition that she did not count, whether consciously or unconsciously, as "influence." Bloom's is one of the few critical evaluations before the new feminist criticism that came close to an accurate assessment of Bogan's place in Anglo-American poetry. His last line opens the way to a consideration of gender and poetry—although Bloom is not conscious of this possibility.

Louise Bogan manipulated the white male tradition to her advantage: By studying and using modernism's lessons, she put herself within the reigning tradition. This was only half of her task; the other was to dissociate herself from the prevailing stereotype of the woman poet, that image of the wailing and uncontrollable poetess of the nineteenth century. Susan Gubar and Sandra Gilbert have pointed out that the woman artist "must confront precursors who are almost exclusively male, and therefore significantly different from her. . . . On the one hand, . . . the woman writer's male precursors symbolize authority; on the other hand, despite their authority, they fail to define the ways in which she experiences her identity as a writer."[25] Bogan used what she could from the male tradition but it had its limits for her, as it does for any woman, since the emotional experience that goes into the poem is *the experience of a woman*. In the next chapter, we will examine Bogan's relationship to the female tradition, that other poetic heritage she had of necessity to confront in her complicated quest for expression.

III.

THE FEMALE HERITAGE
AMBIVALENCE AND RE-VISION

I only ask that a woman be completely
herself and write a work that places her as
a real poet, a real artist, the best of her
kind. Sex is not enough.

—Marya Zaturenska

Certain spectres haunt the minds and talents
of women poets. The first of these are the
Transcendent Figures—for English-speaking
women, Emily Brontë, Christina Rossetti,
and Emily Dickinson. They are also haunted, often to an unrealized degree of
closeness, by the Feminine Terrible Examples, in the persons, of say, Felicia Hemans
and Ella Wheeler Wilcox.

—Louise Bogan, "Verse"

What poetry was one had to learn from the
former poets, most of them men.

—Léonie Adams

Strange trio of my sisters, most diverse,
And how extraordinarily unlike
Each is to me, and which way shall I go?

—Amy Lowell, "The Sisters"

As we have seen, Louise Bogan wanted to be judged in terms of the dominant
poetic movement of her time. As she invoked the modernists and their precursors as her masters, she also had to dissociate herself from prevailing ideas
of the "woman poet." What this chapter will show is how Louise Bogan's
"aesthetic of limitation" was formed in part in response to her interpretation
of the nineteenth-century female tradition. We will see how Bogan's aesthetic
is in part derived from the past; then we will examine how she applied this

aesthetic of limitation to her own generation as she judged their work. Her stance is informed by an extreme ambivalence toward other women, an attitude rooted in her ambivalence about her own womanhood, a confusion perfectly understandable in a social order that devalues women.

When we judge women's contributions to culture without an active consciousness of the social condition of women, we necessarily misjudge. Because her ambivalence affected her assessment of the past, there was much of the tradition of women's poetry that she could not use. What this chapter will show, among other things, is how the literary history of modern women poets is a history of loss. We shall see how a flawed analysis of the renunciation motif of the nineteenth century, incomplete editions of Dickinson, and the late publication and mis-readings of H.D. all contributed to much less than a full view of the tradition of women's poetry. In contrast, men have the entire Western literary canon to draw upon and to contend with as they form their work. To her credit, Louise Bogan was the only modern woman poet to inquire about her foremothers; moreover, as poetry critic of the *New Yorker,* she was highly influential in defining "women's poetry." Because she was a highly conscious writer who thought about "the tradition" and because she wrote so much criticism, we are able to trace her evolving definition of women's poetic capacities. We will see, strikingly, the gradual metamorphosis of Louise Bogan's point of view.

Patriarchy defines women, and women internalize these definitions. We can expect then that a male poet's version of the female heritage will become normative. There is a predictable quality about commentaries on female poets by male poets in the modern period. Any one of us who has delved into assessments of women poets by men knows the elements of the stereotype; Theodore Roethke's characterization in a 1961 review of Louise Bogan is typical, part of a long male line of the denigration of women's art. In this review, Roethke's ultimate purpose is to set Bogan apart from other women poets:

> Two of the charges most frequently levelled against poetry by women are lack of range—in subject matter, in emotional tone—and lack of a sense of humor. And one could, in individual instances among writers of real talent, add other aesthetic and moral shortcomings: the spinning out; the embroidering of trivial themes; a concern with the mere surfaces of life—that special province of the feminine talent in prose—hiding from the real agonies of the spirit; refusing to face up to what existence is; lyric or religious posturing; running between the boudoir and the altar; stamping a tiny foot against God or lapsing into a sententiousness that implies the author has reinvented integrity; carrying on excessively about Fate, about time; lamenting the lot of the woman; caterwauling; writing the same poem about fifty times, and so on. . . . Louise Bogan is something else. True, a very few of her earliest poems bear the mark of fashion, but for the most part she writes out of the severest lyrical tradition in English. Her real spiritual ancestors are Campion, Jonson, the anonymous Elizabethan song writers. . . .[1]

Utterly sarcastic, Roethke invokes history's judgment to bolster his own notion that women lead narrow, insignificant lives; thus it follows that our poems are trivial. The woman poet's tininess (spiritual, physical) is nothing against God (presumably male). We are utterly unlike Roethke who knows "the real agonies of the spirit," who knows, in fact, "what existence is." This condescension and arrogance are familiar; we have heard them many times before. It was this idea of the woman poet that Bogan and her contemporaries had to dismantle. One of their strategies was to dissociate themselves from the prevailing view of women poets. And, in this, according to Roethke, Bogan had succeeded.

Just a year after Roethke published his review, Bogan gave a talk at Bennington College on "the achievement of certain remarkable women writers who were not poets, but novelists, critics and (dreadful word) feminists" (JAR 135). (At this point in her life, Bogan did not object to the ideas of feminists as much as to the label that described them.) In the Bennington talk, Bogan scrupulously avoided extended discussion of *her* genre. But she did warn briefly of women's errors in poetry:

> . . . in the case of the woman writer and particularly of the woman poet, every lie—every fib, even—shows, like a smutch on a child's (or on a woman's) cheek. We can, perhaps, at this point draw up a short list of tentative rules. First, in literature (or in any other art) women must not lie. Second, they must not attitudinize (in the role of the *femme fatale* least of all). And they must neither theatricalize nor coarsen their truths. They must not be vain, and they must not flight or kite in any witch-like way. Nor, on the other hand, go in for little girlishness and false naiveté. Nor "stamp a tiny foot at the universe." (JAR 156)

Of course, this is meant to be funny. (In a letter written two days before she was to deliver her speech, Bogan wrote, "If they don't laugh the first five minutes, I'll just start cutting, as I go along" [JAR 134].) The passage, which ends by quoting Roethke, repeats all the themes he had sounded: Women must search for the truth of existence (not lie), not whine (caterwaul), not exploit their womanliness. Nor stamp our tiny feet! Now, one might assume this is just one more example of a woman poet who internalizes male imperatives. In this case, it is quite likely that Roethke modelled his ideas of women's poetry upon Bogan's, since she was older, a kind of mentor, and much more knowledgeable on the subject.

I first read Bogan's short list of tentative rules in an essay by William Jay Smith. "Louise Bogan: A Woman's Words" (1970) is an affectionate retrospective that quotes from portions of the Bennington address. To know only this passage is to have a skewed view of Bogan's attitudes toward women artists. Not until I saw the text in its entirety, through Ruth Limmer's autobiographical mosaic, did I learn that this half tongue-in-cheek injunction comes at the end of a long piece that is full of pride in the accomplishments of women. Bogan delivered the Bennington speech when she was sixty-five; to write it, she probed into women's history as she had never done before. It is one of her most complete expressions of the achievement and specialness—and limitations—of women. We will look at that Bennington address in greater detail later in this chapter.

For the moment what interests us is that in 1965, her poetic *oeuvre* complete, Bogan was still willing to invoke some of the old ideas—those that dominated in the twenties and thirties—about the pitfalls of being a woman who also wants to be a poet. In 1965 she spoke from a mature vantage point with vast experience as a woman poet and a sense of tradition derived from her reading of women's history. She could now look back upon a generation of women who had challenged the stereotype of the wailing poetess. As we reflect upon the history of women's poetry, we can see that Bogan and her generation, bent on defeating the stereotype and determined to be judged along with the men, paradoxically established a female tradition within the modernist mode. This was a new women's poetry that, according to Bogan, neither exploited woman's natural resource, emotion, nor abandoned it.

Louise Bogan's first book, *Body of This Death,* was published in 1923 when the poet was only twenty-six. It is her most immediate, her most emotional book; her subject is woman's subject, romantic love and disillusionment. (Some of these are the poems that Roethke thought "bear the mark of fashion. . . .") By the time *Body of This Death* was published, Bogan was living in New York City and beginning to find friends in the literary world. She was being asked to write criticism but felt she absolutely must not review other women of her generation who were trying to write poetry. This was partly because she was not yet confident enough as a critic. At the heart of her refusal, however, was a sense of how impossible it was for one woman to speak honestly about the work of another writing woman. All women poets were vulnerable precisely because there were so few of them. In 1929, Bogan wrote to Harriet Monroe, editor of *Poetry* magazine, turning down her request to review a book by a woman whom she had met and who had a volume coming out the same year as Bogan's *Dark Summer.* "I have never tried to review a book of poetry by a woman contemporary. I have seen so much nonsense arising from friendship (or even enmity) between author and reviewer" (12 Oct. 1929, 49). In 1930, she had begun work on a review of Lola Ridge's *Firehead* for *Poetry* but decided not to follow through on it because she could not write a favorable one. As an honest critic, she felt constrained by the sense she always had to praise women; but she was not going to publicly denigrate them either. She wrote to Miss Monroe: "I have found from bitter experience that one woman poet is at a disadvantage in reviewing another, if the review be not laudatory." Bogan was afraid Ridge would take her words "too much to heart"; and she was feeling too vulnerable herself to take this on, for in early 1930 she was contending with the complete destruction of her house by fire. "And since I know that Miss Ridge is ill, and no doubt puts much store by good reviews—I do not feel that you should allow me to go on with my article, since my attitude must be a purely critical one" (17 Jan. 1930, 56).

At the same time she was turning down requests to review women poets, Bogan considered some women poets her friends; she wrote to editors praising the work of some of her contemporaries. The women poets mentioned most often in her letters in the early thirties are Léonie Adams, Genevieve Taggard, and Edna St. Vincent Millay. In an assessment we would today call overblown, she wrote to her own editor in 1929 that Léonie Adams "has the greatest talent in the really grand manner of anyone writing in America today" (12 Oct. 1929, 48). She remained on good terms with Léonie Adams over the years; Adams dedicated *High Falcon* (1929) to Bogan and Raymond Holden. Bogan and her husband socialized with Genevieve ("Jed") Taggard and her husband, Robert Wolf, until Taggard and Wolf accused them of being "habitual drunkards." There are many references to Taggard in the letters, indicating that the two poets continued a relationship that was sometimes friendly, sometimes acrimonious. A final break came in the mid-thirties when Bogan isolated herself from many of her friends because of her refusal to join in left-wing politics—and Taggard wrote a nasty poem about this attitude. "I Sigh If She Were Dying" appeared in 1934 in *Not Mine to Finish:*

> If she were dying in wild leisurely fashion
> Enjoying death with the great bitterness of her nature
> I would be envious of her crowning and eloquent passion
> And write her a message, saying, This is your face your
>
> Last accomplishment; make the most of it.
> She is still frittering and mocking and is still withheld
> From the larger matter of her better wit;
> And I who love her neither killed nor quelled,
>
> Think; we are odd women, the two of us. She is
> the wild nature I mirror but do not have; And I
> Am so the hater of waste that I hunger to kiss
> The horrible face of her life and the clothes of her grave.
>   I sigh.[2]

A bad poem—at moments it does not make any sense; a mean one—mean in the way women learn to be mean to each other; an ambivalent one, as Taggard in the last stanza links the two women, making them two sides of a single nature. As we would expect, Bogan had a poetic answer, lengthily entitled "Lines Written After Detecting in Myself a Yearning Toward the Large, Wise, Calm, Richly Resigned, Benignant Act Put on by a Great Many People After Having Passed the Age of Thirty-five."[3]

A profound change in Louise Bogan's relationship to all poets came with her appointment as a poetry critic of the *New Yorker* in 1931. Bogan complained a great deal about this job: It interfered with her creative life; it reminded her that she was primarily self-taught, not as well-educated, in the formal sense, as most of the people with whom she associated; most important, because she was determined to be "honest," as she saw it, and put "standards" above friendship, it got her into a lot of trouble. In 1931, then, she was forced to take a public stand on poetry; this necessarily included an assessment of women poets. The task no doubt helped her to formulate in a coherent and sustained way her ideas about the special province of women of letters. Her reviews are invaluable to us as a record of one distinguished woman poet's response to American poetry from the twenties through the sixties.

Her strong public stance had a particularly marked effect on her relationships with women. For example, Bogan's reviews of Edna St. Vincent Millay's poems in the late thirties put an end to their friendship; we will discuss this relationship in greater detail later in this chapter. To understand the complexity of friendships and rivalries between "exceptional" white women in New York City in the twenties and the thirties, we need to be acutely aware of historical moment and context. This was the post-suffrage era, the age, in sophisticated circles, of the "free woman."[4] Feminist analyses of the lives of American women in the late twenties and thirties are only now beginning to emerge, but it is surely too simple to say that feminism died utterly after the vote was won; rather, feminism was expressed in different ways, depending on the color, the class, the economic situation and the location of the women involved. In New York, the white, middle-class, upwardly mobile woman saw that it was in her interests to identify publicly more with men than with women. In fact, this point of view is not unlike that of the so-called "post-feminist" generation of the eighties. Elaine Showalter's reissue of *These Modern Women,* essays written for the *Nation* in 1926–27, is a valuable document for understanding one privileged group of women in the twenties. Through the essays, published anonymously and written by successful women, the *Nation* wanted "to discover the origin of their modern point of view toward men, marriage, children and jobs."[5] Showalter writes in the introduction that there is an "absence of any discussion of female relationships" (16) and quotes from a 1927 *Harper's* article in which one woman defined "Feminist—New Style": "She 'freely admits that American women have so far achieved but little in the arts, sciences, and professions as compared with men.' She does not identify with women and prefers to work with men, 'for their methods are more direct, and their view larger, and she finds that she can deal with them on a basis of frank comradeship.' " This view—that relationships with women are too competitive and that men are more compatible and supportive—seems to be common among upwardly mobile women in periods after organized women's movements. Some women in the twenties completely internalized the culture's view of their role while others skillfully negotiated between female and male worlds. That is, sometimes the identification with men was real and paramount; in other cases, it was a conscious strategy. For example, Genevieve Taggard, one of the poets mentioned most often in Bogan's early letters, had a complicated approach to the dilemma of the modern woman poet. A socialist who published a critical biography of Emily Dickinson in 1930, her essay for the *Nation* series focused on the strength of her mother as a role model; yet in the introduction to her *Collected Poems 1918–1938,* she made it clear that she wanted to be judged as a poet, not a poetess:

Many poems in this collection are about the experiences of women. I hope these express all types of candid and sturdy women. . . . All those who try to live richly and intelligently. I have refused to write out of a decorative impulse, because I conceive it to be the dead end of much feminine talent. A kind of literary needlework. I think the later poems and some of the early ones hold a wider consciousness than that colored by the feminine half of the race. I hope they are not written by a poetess, but by a poet. I think, I hope, I have written poetry that relates to the general experience and the realities of the time.[6]

The passage is riddled with all the contradiction and ambivalence typical of ambitious women of this time. Taggard says that women can live richly and intelligently; and she puts women in the human race with poems that assert our humanness. In this way, she can claim that her poems are universal. At the same time, she sets herself apart from many women, as she asserts that most of the female population has not achieved the same breadth of consciousness as the sturdy women she admires. Such denigration shows a lack of profound understanding and empathy for the general situation of women. Bogan shared this individualistic view.

Hindsight tells us that Louise Bogan knew what she was up against as a woman beginning a poetic career in the twenties. Perhaps not immediately—but after the first book was published in 1923, she began to understand even more clearly the limits of the woman poet. Léonie Adams pointed to this conscious awareness in a review of Bogan's work published in 1954:

I wrote a time ago and feel as strongly or more strongly now that hers was an art of limits, the limits of the inner occasion and of the recognized mode. These are formal limits . . . she accepted with some others of the best of her poetic generation that that generation was not to be so abundant as its predecessor, and later within her work as critic she would welcome a generation that would be more abundant again . . . I was not . . . then aware that *she* was so aware that she must function not only as a poet of her own time but within the limits accorded a woman poet. . . .[7]

The recognized mode was modernism, the inner occasion the source of the lyric impulse. Adams explained in a letter to me that the formal limits of which she spoke were "of course that of the lyric, for her as well as for myself."[8] Besides the formal definitions supplied by modernism, there were limits applied specifically to women who would be poets:

There was still at the time not a little of the Matchless Orinda syndrome in readers of women's poetry. It was easy for one of her probity to avoid the mistakes some others had made—those she used to call (after the late Clinch Calkins) the 'O God, the pain girls.' (46)

The passage illustrates a strong sense of some kind of female tradition in poetry—a strong negative sense. "Matchless Orinda," part of a literary circle in seventeenth-century England whose members took pseudonyms, was in fact

Katherine Philips (1631–64), who wrote poetry in which, as Ann Stanford tells us, "passionate love is cast out with the words 'Hence, Cupid, with your cheating toys.' "[9] Such lines would have left Bogan howling. She and her contemporaries came to know "Matchless Orinda" through a volume of her poetry edited by Louise Guiney in 1904. Orinda's contemporary counterpart was Clinch Calkins, a modern exponent of exaggerated emotion. This was the tradition of women's poetry against which Bogan, Adams and others aligned themselves. Adams made further distinctions:

> There could be no confusion of the role of woman and the role of poet, or any exploitation of the role of woman. She knew, moreover, that she should not model herself upon the women she admired and who were closest to her in time. But she read good women writers, contemporaries such as Viola Meynell, who were not poets but writers of prose and noted in them a marvelous delicacy and restraint at employing the female sensibility for the scene. There was no need for a woman to justify this attachment by a philosophy of nature or a metaphysic of angels: she took it for granted. Perhaps to respond effectively to whatever is—the landscape, the room, the scene around—is to love it perceptively, as we love people. This was a part of the feminine way, and one could easily be quite lax and overdo it. In the writers just alluded to, such perceptions were subsidiary to the larger narrative structure, and in the poem she would make them subsidiary to the sequence of unstated statement. Thus, she could achieve the lyric intensity without indulging, because it was natural to her, the true voice of woman's feeling. (46)

These are the hurdles set for women poets. It is telling that Bogan felt she could not look to other women poets as models, that she had to advertise her own original voice. Adams agreed with Bogan that modernist women poets had to avoid overabundant expressions of feeling; for women, form is the clue; the compression of the modern lyric helps women keep feeling in check. In her letter to me, Adams wrote that "while women resemble each other in some matters of sensibility and experience, this is another thing from craft, and the whole sense of the art itself."[10] But how separate form and content and the roles of woman and poet, since we write out of our experience? It is this very tension between an expression of one's life and the imperative that one not write as a "woman poet" that is at the heart of the dilemma of the modernist woman poet. Bogan was more successful than Adams perhaps because she understood the dilemma more deeply—and because she let herself go more. She learned how to keep a kind of terrible balance between the expression of emotion and its control.

Yet we have cause to wonder, as we examine Bogan's relationship to the female tradition, why she aligned herself with those poets now considered relatively "minor"—Léonie Adams, Elinor Wylie, even for a time Edna St. Vincent Millay—while neglecting those presently judged "greater" poets by male critics and by some women critics as well. The reasons are several, as we shall see; but one of them surely has to do with this idea of preserving "the true

voice of woman's feeling" in poetry without indulging it. Bogan's contemporaries, Marianne Moore and Gertrude Stein and H.D., developed their
original voices in virtual isolation, voices quite different from Bogan's; among
the modernist woman poets, hers was perhaps the most purely lyric talent and
temperament. Adams and Millay and Wylie were also devoted to an expression of female emotion; I think Bogan felt more comfortable writing about
these women because she understood their poetic impulse—even though at
moments in her career she disowned it. It is also possible that she did not feel
competitive with them because she believed that hers was the greater talent.

For Bogan's generation, then, the previous female tradition was something
to be overcome. This is yet another reminder of the loss of our own history and
our ambivalence about being women and our sense of competitiveness with
other "successful" women. Bogan, who focused on a conception of the wailing
poetess of the nineteenth century, might have also used the powerful female
poetic tradition of Elizabeth Barrett Browning, Christina Rossetti, Emily
Brontë, and Emily Dickinson. Moreover, her assessment of popular nineteenth-century American women's poetry was off the mark. For example, in
1935, the *New Republic* asked Bogan to do an anthology of poems by women
of her generation. She was clear how she felt about this:

> The point is: Malcolm Cowley, a month or so ago, asked me to edit an
> anthology of female verse, to be used in the pages of the N.R. They have, as you
> know, already published groups of Middle-Western verse, and whatnot. They
> are now about to divide mankind horizontally rather than vertically, sexually
> rather than geographically.—As you might have expected, I turned this pretty
> job down; the thought of corresponding with a lot of female songbirds made me
> acutely ill. It is hard enough to bear with my own lyric side. The idea and the
> task have gone on, however, to Hildegard Flanner, and she has written me
> asking for an immediate contribution. (1 July 1935, 86)

Bogan makes the point with characteristic good humor—and plenty of visceral
disgust—as she separates herself from the stereotype of the woman poet who
lets her feelings get the better of her. By an unbearable "lyric side," she means
an overindulgence in feeling; "mawkish" was another expression she used to
describe some of the poems she decided not to publish. In the same letter, she
admits to "falling mildly in love with an enormous young man from Ann
Arbor, Mich." The young man was Theodore Roethke and "I found myself
writing the most extraordinary Ella Wheeler Wilcoxism, as a consequence.
This last will never be seen by human eye, I trust. Never shall I give the
feminine sonneteers any competition. O, I'm a strange one, amen't I." Ella
Wheeler Wilcox was associated in Bogan's mind with the Matchless Orinda/
Clinch Calkins school of poetry; she characterizes her in a 1947 essay as "the
Wisconsin farm girl, who spiced her stanzas with hints of sin in *Poems of
Passion* (1883) but soon quiets down into marriage and respectability with a
Mr. Wilcox" (PA 427). Bogan came to feel some kind of an obligation to

publicly denounce this aspect of the female heritage and this impulse was encouraged by a male friend and critic, Edmund Wilson. She wrote to Katharine White of the *New Yorker* in 1936:

> E. Wilson has fallen heir to some Victorian anthologies, or garlands, of female poetry, and he thought it would be a good idea if I did a piece on same, linking them up with modern female verse, the point being that when the girls had a restricted life, they were far more ardent, lauding the virtues of husbands and connubial bliss in general in far from uncertain terms; while modern female verse tends to vilify and belittle the masculine charms, much of it being written just after or just before some disillusion handed to the woman by the man. Do you think this idea would mean anything to the magazine? The Victorian quotations are howls, I can assure you. (5 Feb. 1936, 126)

It was precisely this contrast between dependent and independent females which came to interest Bogan as she reviewed the nineteenth-century tradition. Wilson had had his own experience with the independence of those modern poetesses, Millay and Bogan; he had an affair with Millay and wanted more than a close friendship with Bogan.

Bogan's article, "Poetesses in the Parlor," was based on her reading of Rufus Griswold's influential anthology *Female Poets of America* (1859) and *Love Poems of Three Centuries* (1890), edited by Jessie F. O'Donnell. Her ironic title points to the idea of nineteenth-century women's poetry held by the twentieth century. The essay begins with Bogan's sarcastic humor: "In whatever coarse surroundings American female poetry is destined to decay, its initial triumphs occurred in the parlor."[11] By this Bogan means both the appropriation of literature by the bourgeoisie and the fact that in contrast to the English tradition, women of all classes in America wrote poetry. Of working-class background herself, Bogan could not have found this fact entirely unappealing. The essay moves through moods of irony and sarcasm, is at moments tongue-in-cheek, but occasionally slips into real involvement and sympathy for the strategies of these nineteenth-century women. In the O'Donnell anthology, Bogan found "the real emotional gems of the female verse of this period" (48). She sees a difference between the love poetry of women and men: "The feminine contributors positively seethe with feeling, while the passive attitude has to some extent been taken over by the males. It is the masculine voice which now assumes the tones of nostalgia and yearning, and the feminine that hymns the unfettered joys of the here-and-now" (48–49). Among these poems, she finds some critical of the marriage bond; she is pleased when she discovers that mawkishness is not the only mode and "a healthy assertiveness" appears: "The voice of women waiting and weeping are pretty well covered by women's voices doing nothing of the sort" (49). (Bogan wrote this review about a year after ending her second and last marriage.) She praises the "woman scorned, who contrary to previous habit, now has her own remarks to make about her situation" (49).

As a modern woman, Bogan was surprised to find assertiveness in these poems, since a renunciation motif does predominate in them. In fact, she dismissed much of the earlier verse because it reminded her too much of some of her own tendencies. "It is hard enough to bear with my own lyric side," she had written in turning down the *New Republic* anthology of women poets (1 July 1935, 86). "My own ideas are steeped in a romantic brew, however much I hate the color and the stain," she wrote in 1933 (JAR 78). Yet, as Cheryl Walker vividly shows in *The Nightingale's Burden,* that poetry of renunciation and ambivalence written by Elizabeth Oakes Smith, Maria Brooks, and Frances Osgood was not entirely unlike the work of Bogan, Millay, and Wylie.[12] Like every history we do not know, this one was bound to be repeated. What Walker shows is the cost of denying the nineteenth-century heritage, of mythologizing it, of not seeing it clear and whole, for in effect, twentieth-century women poets re-invented the wheel, obsessed as they were with some of the same themes of ambivalence and renunciation that had preoccupied the earlier generation. For Walker, Bogan is a particularly vivid example of the link to this tradition. Walker points to the "value of stifling parts of the self" exemplified by "Henceforth, From the Mind" and the identification of maturity with resignation, present in many of Bogan's poems, as well as the self-destruction that cuts off a move toward power, and thus reflects an ambivalence toward it ("The Dragonfly") and the stereotype of a woman's special sensibility, which can lead her to the brink of madness, as in "I Saw Eternity." Walker's analysis is successful in linking these two traditions. Although many of the themes are the same, they do come out of a different consciousness in the modern period. When Bogan resigns herself to an end to romantic love, she does so after a great deal of experience and the knowledge that it is not her only option, for she is an independent woman; the nineteenth-century poet most often renounces freedom and accepts her "fetters." Yet each renunciation is an expression of the limitations of being a woman in a patriarchal culture.

Further, "Poetesses in the Parlor" is enlightening because it is one of the first explicit indications that Bogan subscribed to the nineteenth-century idea of "the separate spheres," that is, that women and men are innately different. In a 1961 letter Bogan would say that "nature meant men to be radiantly intellectual (when they are gifted). Women tap the lifeforce more successfully at other levels" (4 Nov. 1961, 335). As she worked on her 1936 essay, it was the introduction in Griswold which impressed her:

> . . . he makes a pronouncement full of real insight, which his contributors no doubt passed over without turning a hair. "It is less easy to be assured of the genuineness of literary ability in women than in men. We are in danger of mistaking for the efflorescent energy of creative intelligence that which is only the exuberance of 'feelings unemployed.' " (45)

We know from Léonie Adams that Bogan thought women poets must avoid indulging the feeling side that was natural to them; she took a less negative view of women's feeling in poetry in later years. In 1936 she agreed with Griswold. She had also read his elaboration of the point about the woman poet's defects:

> We may confound the vivid dreamings of an unsatisfied heart with the aspirations of a mind impatient of the fetters of time, and matter, and mortality. That may seem to us the abstract imagining of a soul rapt into sympathy with a purer beauty and a higher truth than earth and space exhibit which in fact shall be only the natural craving of affectations, undefined and wandering.[13]

The prose is decidedly nineteenth century but the point of view is much like Theodore Roethke's: Men possess the capacity for abstract lofty thought while women are "hiding from the real agonies of spirit" and engaging in "lyric or religious posturing." Women write, Griswold seems to say, when they have nothing better to do, when their emotions have no object. Bogan found examples for this in the anthology: "We turn to the body of the book and almost at once come upon Margareta V. Bleecker (1771–1801), who, when 'relieved of her wastral husband's presence by the yellow fever,' immediately wrote 'Belisarius,' a tragedy in five acts" (45). However, Bogan shows more empathy than Griswold, as she goes on to point out how many women wrote because they were widows or had husbands who were financial failures. Her essay ends with some ambivalence and a strong dose of sarcasm: "For future good or ill, something remarkable had happened in the parlor" (52).

We are left with the impression that Bogan empathized with some aspects of the nineteenth-century tradition and felt that modern women poets could learn something from it. Most important, the essay establishes Bogan's standard of measurement for women's poetry: Does it avoid sentimentality? Bogan wanted feeling in women's poetry to come out of strength, to be disciplined. Three months after the publication of "Poetesses in the Parlor," Edmund Wilson again encouraged Bogan to take on the women; he "drew up a list of American women writers he thinks I should do a series of pieces on—but I am rather cold to the prospect" (10 April 1936, 129). Despite Wilson's urgings, despite her primary identification with men and male poets, Bogan still remained ambivalent about taking women to task publicly. But when books of verse by women came out, especially those by prominent poets such as Edna St. Vincent Millay, she could not avoid a review. In 1937, the same year her third volume, *The Sleeping Fury,* appeared, Bogan was worrying over a negative review of Millay's latest book. She wrote to her friend Theodore Roethke:

> The new Edna Millay book, *Conversation at Midnight,* is enough to make the angels weep. I must polish it off, critically, next week. I feel terrible about having to do it, for I must say what I think, and she was once a very close and generous friend to me.—Why she had to write this doggerel, I can't think. . . . (12 July 1937, 157)

"Standards," honesty, before friendship; there is something absolutist, inflexible about such a stance. Bogan was even more direct about *Conversation at Midnight* in a letter to her confidant, Wilson: "It's certainly regression: back to the smartiness of high school debates, wherein each kid tried to *sound* more profound than the other. And better-read. And more blasé. And more snobby . . ." (27 July 1937, 158). In earlier days Wilson had shown Millay some of Bogan's poems and Millay had responded with great enthusiasm: "Who is this person? I never even heard of her. I was quite thrilled by some of the poems. Isn't it wonderful how the lady poets are coming along? 'Votes for women' is what I sez!"[14]

The allusion to the feminist movement and thus to a community of women with common problems and goals is crucial here. Millay felt this connection and felt it in a political way; Bogan did not. Louise Bogan's evaluation of her generation's most popular woman poet, Edna St. Vincent Millay, is the most stunning example of Bogan's role as arbiter of standards for poetry by women. Three principles underlie her critique. First, she was simply disappointed in Millay, because she felt she had not lived up to her lyric promise. Second, she abhorred her political poetry as she detested the public pronouncements in verse of men of letters. Third, and most important, she felt Millay had not "grown up." Her long review of *Conversation at Midnight* in the *New Yorker* is strong, energetic and sarcastic:

> Edna Millay, longer than a good many of her contemporaries, held off from getting into the arena and hurling around opinions and exhortations, mixing it up in an argumentative way. It seemed to be her conviction, up to a short time ago, as it was Goethe's, that the artist should not be entirely the pupil of his age. She had opinions, and stated them, with courage, but song came first. The fine line written down in the strength of feeling, with her, was important, in a time made queer by, among other causes, its inability to face emotion and see it through.
>
> Directly after having given us her "Epitaph for the Race of Man," she has written *Conversation at Midnight,* which is an argument. It is an argument which gets nowhere. . . .[15]

The original version of "Conversation at Midnight" was lost in a fire; the rewritten poem is in fact an unpoetic and tedious argument about capitalism and communism between a group of men of various classes and political persuasions.[16] Bogan's contempt for it was shared by many critics. Her review points up her belief in the necessary separation of the private and the public worlds: she felt that an exclusive involvement in the public world prevents a coming-to-terms with emotion. Moreover, she believed it was crucial for women above all to bring emotion—albeit controlled emotion—to the poetry of the thirties. As Susan Schweik points out, Millay "consciously defined her Second War propaganda poems as ephemera, and emphasized their local and temporary quality with several strategies: by calling them 'not poems, posters'; and by marking, through visual differences in printing, their deviation from her 'real,' high literary work."[17] Between 1925 and 1939, Millay published a number of political poems, including "Justice Denied in Massachusetts," on the Sacco and Vanzetti trial, and the sonnet sequence "Epitaph for the Race of Man." According to Sharon Mayer Libera,

> When the war actually came, she turned poetry to a thinner propaganda, and afterward blamed on this episode a serious nervous breakdown, in 1944, from which she seems never completely to have recovered. She wrote apologetically to Edmund Wilson: "For five years I had been writing almost nothing but propaganda. And I can tell you from my own experience, that there is nothing on this earth which can so much get on the nerves of a good poet, as the writing of bad poetry. Anyway, finally, I cracked up under it. I was in the hospital a long time."[18]

While we cannot defend many of Millay's anti-war poems on artistic grounds, the present generation is much more sympathetic with her move to claim some "public space" for woman's voice; and we are also more attuned to some of the ambivalences and conflicts she herself felt about this political role.[19] In 1940, after quickly producing *Make Bright the Arrows,* Millay wrote to a friend, "I have one thing to give in the service of my country,—my reputation as a poet."[20]

Louise Bogan's review in 1939 of *Huntsman, What Quarry?* is even more illuminating for its declaration of what a woman poet must accomplish (PA 298–99). In it, Bogan expresses the view that Millay's 1934 volume, *Wine from These Grapes,* "showed signs of Miss Millay's successful passage from the emotions and point of view of a rebellious girl to those of a maturely contemplative woman." This sounds like an older woman speaking of a younger one, but Millay was in fact five years older than Bogan. These feelings must be seen in the context of Bogan's own struggles, culminating in *The Sleeping Fury* (1937), when Bogan felt she had reached some sense of resolution and calm about the conflicts of her youth and a more balanced, if not resigned, attitude toward romantic love. She found *Huntsman* "a strange mixture of maturity and unresolved youth" and lamented the effects of popularity ("It is a dangerous lot, that of the charming, romantic public poet, especially if it falls to a woman.") She thinks this public adulation has encouraged Millay to keep writing the same kinds of poems, has prevented her from growing up:

> It is difficult to say what a woman poet should concern herself with as she grows older, because women who have produced an impressively bulky body of work are few. But is there any reason to believe that a woman's spiritual fibre is less sturdy than a man's? Is it not possible for a woman to come to terms with herself, if not the world; to withdraw more and more, as time goes on, her own personality from her productions, to stop childish fears of death and eschew charming rebellions against facts. . . . (PA 299)

I hear the resignation motif here, the voice of a woman who has been sorely disappointed and is trying to adjust her expectations of life. Bogan's review ends with these words:

> . . . what has happened to the kind of development announced in *Wine from These Grapes,* the most kindly disposed reader cannot say. If Miss Millay should give up for good the idea that 'wisdom' and 'peace' are stuffy concepts, perhaps that development might be renewed. (PA 299)

Even as Bogan praised Elinor Wylie for "mature emotional richness" and Léonie Adams for her ability "to escape from the atmosphere of modishness that clung in some degree to the work of Miss Millay and Mrs. Wylie," her final word on Millay, in *Achievement in American Poetry, 1900–1950* (1951), was that

> A certain hampering nihilism, as well as a close attachment to literary fashion . . . prevented her from breaking through to impressive maturity; but even her later work is filled with distinguished fragments . . . that she was, by nature, a lyric poet of the first order, is an incontestable fact. (AA 79–80)

We would agree today with elements of Bogan's evaluation, since "The Ballad of Chaldon Down," "The Princess Recalls Her One Adventure," and "Song for Young Lovers in a City" (all in *Huntsman, What Quarry?*) are rather childish. Yet there are some real gems in Millay's oeuvre, including many insightful poems about the experience of women. In retrospect, one wishes that Bogan had been able to be more sensitively empathic with the trials of another woman poet rather than setting herself apart from her; however, it is often the case that women are much harder on other women than any man would be. Bogan saw her own conflicts mirrored in the work of her women contemporaries. When, in her 1939 review of Millay, she wonders what a woman should write about as she grows older, she is expressing her own fears. When she writes in 1951 of "impressive maturity," she is thinking back to confrontations with her psychic demons in the thirties. She is, above all, prescribing her own rigid "aesthetic of limitation" for others. Whatever might be said of Millay, one cannot claim that she had a hard time writing or finding subjects for poetry; Bogan, on the other hand, wrote less and less as she grew older because she no longer had access to her major subject—romantic love. Her command that Millay, that a woman poet must, like a man, rise to the occasion of maturity and "withdraw . . . her own personality from her productions" demands to be seen in the context of a famous man's prescription: "The progress of an artist . . . is . . . a continual extinction of personality."[21] With critical distance, we know just how much "personality" reposes in T. S. Eliot's moving modern poems; nor did Eliot take his own directives to their literal extreme, "giving in" (as Bogan would have seen it) to the comforts of organized religion. What I am suggesting here is that men have much more latitude than women no matter the aesthetic: Within the large oeuvre of an Eliot or a Yeats, there are "bad" poems. Critics do not seem to go out of their way to point these out as they do with Millay.

A decided shift in tone toward the subject "women's poetry" emerged in Louise Bogan's criticism in the late forties, as she developed a theory of women's special gift. She was fifty when she published "The Heart and the Lyre," her first important essay on the female tradition to mirror her slowly shifting perspective on the value of women's "heart" in poetry—a perspective carved out of experience. First, Bogan was able to look back upon the work of some of her contemporaries and to map their contribution to the development of a new idea of women's poetic capacities. Second, her own work was almost complete: After 1947 she would publish only ten more poems. Now she could survey the poetic landscape from a greater distance, one less tied to her own struggles to write. Third, the poetry establishment changed in the forties; it brought with it the poetic logicians, as Bogan called them, and she was distressed by this trend in American poetry. Finally, the world had experienced another war and, although no political creature in the usual sense of that word, Bogan was sensitive to the general feeling of gloom in the creative and intellectual worlds.

I wish now to turn to the writing that marks Bogan's turn toward a favorable evaluation of the female tradition of poetry, including "The Heart and the Lyre" (1947); selected chapters in *Achievement in American Poetry, 1900–1950* (1951); a review of three women poets, "In Balance" (1959); a speech at Bennington, "What the Woman Said"; and a final review, "No Poetesses Maudites" (1963). In these essays, it is as though the ambivalence about being a woman—an ambivalence that had plagued her throughout her writing career—begins to fall away.

"The Heart and the Lyre" (PA 424–29) takes the point of view that women's poetry is valuable because it is centered in feeling; and Bogan warns women poets in the forties against abandoning their natural emotional resources. She suggests that women poets have a harder time than men in establishing a true poetic voice, so sensitive are we to expectations from the world around us. Thus, the fulsome tradition of the nineteenth century found women at its most sentimental edges; on the other hand, women in the forties were moving dangerously close to an exaggerated imitation of intellect in poetry. In "The Heart and the Lyre" Bogan announced her intention to survey American women's poetry but first she turned to "look at some of the assumptions and prejudices that have long lodged in people's minds on the subject of women as poets" (425). "One rather hoary idea," writes Bogan, "is that women put emotion before form and are likely to be indifferent technicians" (425). She points to what was true in her own case: "Do they not usually, as well, imitate closely the poetic productions of men?" (425). That imitation, as we have suggested, was sometimes salutary; Bogan felt that modernism helped her correct her romantic tendencies but it could also lead women down false paths. Having dispensed with the idea that women's poetry is always over-emotional, Bogan reviews its history, reiterating the argument of her 1936 essay, that the earliest American women versifiers were "unendowed, grim, pious and lachrymose" but that toward the end of the century women's poetry got better: "We are now in a new world. The more depressing ante-bellum aspects of female piety and melancholy have worn off, and we are presented with the spectacle of women becoming ever more ardent and airy" (426). In Edmund Clarence Stedman's *An American Anthology* (1900), there are some distinctive voices (". . . if we search carefully for even the smallest sincerity and talent, personalities begin to emerge" [426]). Bogan's prose then artfully mirrors the burial by the female tradition of the greatest American woman poet of the nineteenth century:

> . . . further back, crowded in with Ms. Spofford, Mrs. Moulton . . . we come upon an unpretentious name, easily overlooked, of a woman born in 1830 and dead in 1886: Emily Dickinson. Emily Dickinson represents the final flowering of a long Puritan tradition. Her genius has a hard, bitter kind of civilization behind it; women poets share with men the need for some sort of civilized ground from which to draw sustenance. (427)

The tracing of "civilization," that sense of art's intellectual and spiritual roots, is the raison d'être of Bogan's literary criticism. When in 1939 she had spoken of influences and of her late discovery of Henry James, she associates with him the idea of "civilization and great art," meaning "complexity rather than simplification," "the humane defined as the well-understood because the well-explored. . . ."[22] In "The Heart and the Lyre" she locates Dickinson's civilization in Puritan heritage, the "hard" and "bitter" which is a product of her milieu. These adjectives are striking, attached as they are to a "spinster" woman/poet. Despite the praise of this passage, we still have to contend with Bogan's ambivalence about Emily Dickinson, an ambivalence that may even suggest an underlying rivalry. It is possible that Bogan had not yet noticed Dickinson as she wrote her first book. Yet after that she could not have remained untouched by the judgment of her contemporaries that Dickinson was a genius, a great poet, in fact the only great American woman poet of the nineteenth century. Despite a revival of Dickinson's popularity in the twenties and thirties, that era possessed only the most incomplete view of Dickinson's achievement. This fact was lamented by Bogan's sometime friend, Genevieve Taggard, who wrote a biography of Dickinson published in 1930:

> Some dependable life of Emily Dickinson should have been written thirty-five years ago when her poetry first encountered fame; now, a hundred years after her birth, we realize our loss. Only a small number of the twelve hundred poems catalogued in 1892 have been published. . . .[23]

Bogan may have seen one of the late nineteenth-century editions of Dickin-son's poems or the 1914 edition; I think it more likely that she first became conscious of Dickinson's achievement through the selections edited by Martha

Dickinson Bianchi and Alfred Leete Hampson in 1924, 1926, and 1929.[24] Although these editions were incomplete and some poems were altered, the artfulness and profundity still spoke to her, as they spoke to her generation. In any case, once Bogan discovered Dickinson, she was predictably ambivalent. What she does not say about her is as telling as the major public evaluations, three essays published after the flowering of her own career, in 1945, 1955, and 1959. From these one learns that Bogan was at first taken in by the child/spinster persona Dickinson calculatedly promoted. Dickinson, as Susan Gubar and Sandra Gilbert have formulated it, solved "the problem of being a woman by refusing to admit that she was a woman."[25] In the sexually "free" milieu of New York in the twenties, this persona was a little quaint.

If Dickinson was for Bogan a strong, conscious influence, she is quiet about it. Like Eliot, who sent us down some false paths with analyses of his "objective" poetry, Bogan in her public pronouncements does not lead us to a comparison with Dickinson. In 1939, she had listed her literary "influences" and then hid Dickinson in among fiction writers she kept reading ("The American writers to whom I return are Poe (the Tales), Thoreau, E. Dickinson and Henry James").[26] Yet Marya Zaturenska and Horace Gregory in their *History of American Poetry* (1942)—a book Bogan hated—directly link Dickinson and Bogan: "Miss Bogan published her first book, *Body of This Death*, in 1923, which was at the height of a popular rediscovery of Emily Dickinson and the merits of the seventeenth-century 'metaphysical' poets."[27] In fact, Bogan's second book, *Dark Summer* (1929) has a more 'metaphysical' cast than any of her others, in the sense of grappling with poetry's grand subjects, Time, Life, Death. A poem such as "I Saw Eternity" (50) in that volume could be traced to Dickinson and the female tradition she redefined. Bogan was particularly proud of this poem: "I am sending you a poem that I do not hesitate to claim as mine. In fact I think it one of the most remarkable works ever penned" (To Edmund Wilson, 22 Nov. 1928, 39). She wrote to Ruth Benedict: "To think that I should come, at the age of thirty-one, to the stage where I write poems about Eternity!" (1 Dec. 1928, 39, n3). The rhyme of this note may be a clue to Dickinson's inspiration; moreover, "I Saw Eternity" is different enough in tone and form from other poems in *Dark Summer* to suggest that it may be modelled upon the work of a most admired female predecessor.

But in the thirties Louise Bogan pointed out her relationship to the male modernists: This was her official, her public stance. When she did discover Dickinson, she may have felt at once distrustful of the spinster persona, a little jealous of the art—and at the same time grateful for the permission it gave to write contained, enigmatic poetry about women's experience. The constricted, elliptical form of Dickinson's verse is her announcement of the impossibility in the nineteenth century of being both a woman, as the culture defined it, and a poet/thinker. Louise Bogan gives us a modern version of woman's cryptic condensation, a world in little. Her compacted forms, her suppressions and obscurities, are her declaration of the near impossibility—even in the twentieth century—of being both woman and poet. What she came to understand was that the modernist male credo had to be interpreted differently by women; and perhaps it was Emily Dickinson who helped her to understand this difference between the male and female interpretations of a tradition. For both poets discovered that in limitation lies possibility.

In "The Heart and the Lyre" Bogan goes on to speak of the liabilities and the particular talents of the contemporary generation of women poets. She had appreciated Emily Dickinson for the "civilization" of her work, particularly since

> . . . it is apparently more difficult for women to throw off the more superficial fashions of any society in which they find themselves. The early history of women poets in America should stand as a warning to modern young women of talent. The special virtues of women are clear, in the same record. Women are forced to become adult. They must soon abandon sustained play, in art or life. They are not good at abstractions and their sense of structure is not large; but they often have the direct courage to be themselves. They are practical, intense, and (usually) both generous and magnanimous. They often have a true contemplative gift; and they are natural singers. They are capable of originality and breadth of emotional and intellectual reference as soon as their background opens to any breadth and variety. They are often forced to waste their powers in an inadequate milieu, in social improvisation; to tack back and forth between revolt and conservatism. . . . (427–28)

These are by now the familiar themes of Bogan's literary criticism: women are easily taken in by poetic fads (Millay was Bogan's central example of this predilection); they must renounce "play" early on because it leads to frivolity and superficiality (Bogan's, then Roethke's point). What is different is that now Bogan praises women's "natural" qualities: The emphasis is on our heart. While we are capable of "intellectual reference" (if we are exposed to education and civilization), abstraction is not our strength. On this point, Bogan was always conflicted. She did not think it was woman's nature to be intellectual yet she herself enjoyed "the sense of structure" she associates with thinking. In her sixties, as she worked on a lecture on women to be delivered at Bennington College, Bogan wrote about how hard it was for her to write criticism at first but how much she learned from it. She had always associated intellectual work with male capacities; in 1962 she was ready to admit that she enjoyed it as well:

> . . . the thought struck me that I should take notes happily all my life, not ever troubling to put them into form. I am a woman, and "fundamental brainwork," the building of logical structures, the abstractions, the condensations, the comparisons, the reasonings, *are not expected of me.* But it is only when I am making at least an imitation of such a structure that I am really happy. It is only when the notes fall into form, when the sentences make *at least the sound of style,* that my interest really holds. (JAR 133)

She was perhaps not clear about this point as she wrote "The Heart and the Lyre" in 1947. In this essay, even as she praises our nature and points to our capacity, much of the definition is cast in negative terms: Bogan underlines what we are not, what we cannot do, how we must limit ourselves. Yet in this passage she makes explicit the place of women in a social world that has a profound impact on our development. In other words, she makes it clear that she understands how hard it is for women to find our true voices in a culture that gives us few advantages, that we make many mistakes and suffer through many false starts before we find our place.

Bogan then praises the achievement of several of her contemporaries. "Far from imitating men to an untoward degree," women, she says, "often experiment boldly with form and language" (428). Bogan wants to underline the variety of women's work and their capacity for originality. She goes out of her way to praise several formal innovators—H.D., Gertrude Stein, and Marianne Moore—even though she never really took to their work. But the public point—that women are making a significant contribution to the poetic heritage—is important to her. "Early in the twentieth century," she writes, "Gertrude Stein, working indefatigably and alone, begins to examine words with the detached interest of the scientist and arrange them in abstract patterns." (Yet this is surely not the "heart" that Bogan asks women to bring to poetry.) Of H.D.'s mysticism and obscurity and Marianne Moore's removal from the human, Bogan had much to say publicly and privately. Here, however, for the sake of an idea, the idea of an honorable female tradition, their qualities, rather than their misdemeanors, are given emphasis: "A little later H.D. gives back to Greek themes some of the pure severity of Greek poetry in the original. Marianne Moore applies a naturalist's eye to objects of art and of nature. . . ." She praises these poets whose approaches to poetry she often judged to be too experimental, too intellectual, even as she warns younger women poets against the rationality and technical virtuosity of some of the influential male poets of the forties. Then she unearths an expression that she had abandoned many years before—romantic—and gives it new meaning:

> Young women writing poetry at present are likely to consider the figure of the woman poet as romantic rebel rather ridiculous and outmoded. The youngest generation of women poets is, in fact, moving toward an imitation of certain masculine "trends" in contemporary poetry. They are imitating, moreover, the work of male verbalizers and poetic logicians. . . . The fear of regression into typical romantic attitudes is, at present, operating from feminine talent; and this is not a wholly healthy impulse, for it negates too strongly a living and valuable side of woman's character. In women, more than in men, the intensity of their emotions is the key to the treasures of the spirit. (428)

It is as though Louise Bogan would have it all ways. When the image of the sentimental woman poet dominated in the twenties and thirties—through the nineteenth-century heritage and the popularity of Millay—Bogan called for control to be achieved through form; in the forties, as the winds changed and new poetic modes were dominant, she asked women to bring heart back to verse. We can almost see Bogan standing at Poetry's crossroads, directing the flow of traffic so that control and expressiveness are maintained in perfect balance. Her expectations for women's role in keeping this balance are enormous. The younger generation, she advises, must not look to male poets but rather be inspired by those exemplars of female poetry after 1918: Sara Teasdale, Edna St. Vincent Millay (when she was good), Elinor Wylie, and Léonie Adams. The essay ends in emotional crescendo:

> The great importance of keeping the emotional channels of a literature open has frequently been overlooked. The need of the refreshment and the restitution of feeling, in all its warmth and depth, has never been more apparent than it is today, when cruelty and fright often seem about to overwhelm man and his world. For women to abandon their contact with, and their expression of, deep and powerful emotional streams, because of contemporary pressures, or mistaken self-consciousness, would result in an impoverishment not only of their own inner resources but of mankind's at large. Certainly it is not a regression to romanticism to remember that women are capable of perfect and poignant song; and that when this song comes through in its high and rare form, the result has always been regarded not only with delight but with a kind of awe. It is a good thing for young women to bring to mind the fact that lost fragments of the work of certain women poets—of Emily Dickinson no less than of the Sappho quoted by Longinus as an example of 'the sublime'—are searched for less with the care and eagerness of the scholar looking for bits of shattered human art, than with the hungry eyes of the treasure hunter, looking for some last grain of a destroyed jewel. Though she may never compose an epic or a tragic drama in five acts, the woman poet has her singular role and precious destiny. And at the moment, in a time lacking in truth and certainty and filled with anguish and despair, no woman should be shamefaced in attempting to give back to the world, through her work, a portion of its lost heart. (428–29)

The image of the destroyed jewel is striking; this is a loss almost sexual in its power. The reference to epic and drama is a swipe at Woolf, and perhaps at H.D. Earlier in the essay, Bogan had expounded on *A Room of One's Own* yet strangely missed one of its points ("It was a little old-fashioned even in 1929 for Mrs. Woolf to choose a five-act poetic play as the final test of a woman poet's powers" (425). Again, even as she movingly asks women to bring heart back to poetry, she defines them in terms of limitation. But the difference is that woman's natural quality, "heart," once a liability, is now an asset. Here, miraculously, the female gift is not only good but redemptive—not just for poetry but for the whole race.

This idea of the nature of women's poetry also informed Bogan's brief notices in the *New Yorker,* where she did not hesitate to dismiss the work of women poets who did not in her view represent the possibilities of female talent. For example, she wrote relatively little about H.D., either in the letters, as they are edited, or in her criticism. Because of the lack of critical attention, H.D. almost disappeared to the American public after her imagist phase, since she was living abroad; much of her work went out of print quickly and was not available to a wide audience until the early seventies. Bogan wrote brief, caustic notes about the *Trilogy*. Since she did not think women could be epic poets and because she did not like poetry that depended on allusion—twenty years before, she had made fun of Eliot's notes to *The Waste Land*—we would not expect her to be sympathetic to the *Trilogy*. The tone of the reviews also leads us to believe there was something more personal behind them. In 1928 Bogan told Ruth Benedict of her worries about Léonie Adams, abroad on a Guggenheim: "Léonie writes of H.D.'s teas, Bryher, and Robert McAlmon. I wish she'd see someone more robust" (11 Oct. 1928, 37). One wonders if this disapproval of a certain brand of aestheticism does not serve to mask Bogan's jealousy of a writer who did not have to make a living, and who had time for teas; she felt jealous of Virginia Woolf for the same reason. May Sarton says that Bogan was particularly depressed about her own work in this period: ". . . I know from things Louise said to me later that there was a time of near despair in the '40s when none of her books were in print. For a writer to be unobtainable by readers is, of course, like being buried alive."[28] In 1944 Bogan wrote a review of women poets for her "Verse" column: "The reason may or may not be the war," she begins, but the year saw a number of volumes by women. Although she does not think that "women should be dealt with critically in isolation in any department of art," this outpouring prompts several observations. First, she sees that "Transcendent Figures" such as Emily Brontë, Christina Rossetti, and Emily Dickinson and "Terrible Examples" (Felicia Hemans, Ella Wheeler Wilcox) "haunt the minds and talents of women poets." She goes on to say what she had said many times before—that women are particularly in danger of giving in to fashion and that they must "be able to see around their situation on all sides, and to rise above their time, if their work is not to resemble, after twenty years or so, the dated illustrations in a household magazine." These generalizations are followed by tolerant short notices on the work of Muriel Rukeyser, Babette Deutsch, and Marguerite Young. The review ends with an appraisal of H.D.:

> Finally, in this autumn's list of women, we find H.D., an older figure and a classic of the Imagist school. Some years ago her manner dwindled into smallness and artificiality. Her new book, "The Walls Do Not Fall," based on Egyptian symbolism and concerned with bombed London, shows tenser feeling, writing of more energy, and thought of a larger sweep than has been usual in her poetry for many years.[29]

Four days later Marianne Moore sent Bogan's review of women poets to H.D., with whom she corresponded regularly:

Oct. 29, 1944

Here is a poverty-stricken sheaf of reviews which will tell you more of the abysmal state of criticism in America than it will about your book. I have had several seizures of imaginative apoplexy as I read these over—Muriel's book too has simply not been read. Louise Bogan who was once a fine poet has not survived menopause, I take it, and has become a rabid anti-feminist and self-hater in consequence—her review is simply pathological. I hear that she drinks a great deal. But nothing excuses this sort of thing to my mind. Not content with treating fine poets with the condescension of a Bishop whose ring is being kissed, she must cast ashes at the Comtesse de Noailles. . . . God knows Anna de Noailles has faults but she was *The* romantic poet par excellence and I do not think that her apotheosis of gardens smelled of the Casino. And, for God's sake, are we still in the dark ages that "female poets" are considered a race apart, a port of monsters to be reviewed as such? There is not a spark of generosity in Bogan apparently. She is unable any longer to *rejoice,* poor woman![30]

Moore's perception of the relationship between anti-feminism and self-hate seems extraordinary in her era. Relationships between women in her time were an intricate and intense web of jealousies, rivalries, and alliances; we are not free of these complications today, but we do have the advantage of a developed feminist analysis of them.

To be fair to Bogan, we must report that H.D. considered herself a better poet than many other women who were her contemporaries. Barbara Guest writes that "privately, she [H.D.] considered herself and Moore far superior to other women poets such as Elinor Wylie, Edna St. Vincent Millay, or Sara Teasdale."[31] Marianne Moore supported H.D.'s work—she seems to have been an advocate in the United States for the exiled poet. At moments, Bogan praised Moore. For example, a few months earlier, in April 1944, she had written a long letter to Morton Zabel arguing her choices for the Harriet Monroe Poetry Award. Here one can feel her sureness as a literary critic and her sense of her power and influence. She begins by saying in this private letter that "Marianne represented a decadence, instead of a freshness, of American literature," but after explaining why she thought Robert Penn Warren, John Peale Bishop, Horace Gregory, Delmore Schwartz, Randall Jarrell, Karl Shapiro, and James Agee should not get the prize, she comes out strongly for Moore:

> . . . [T]o turn back to poets over 40: I certainly think it should be Marianne, in spite of the remarks I have taken pains to make, above. She represents, decadence or no, the high formal line that needs to be stressed and helped. She should have received every prize in America, long ago, including the Pulitzer and anything the Am. Acad. of A. and Letters had to hand out. She has developed, and writes more beautifully now (in the last book) than she ever did. She has a spiritual side, in working order (to put it crassly!) She is really, as you say, a sort of saint of American poetry; and although I feel that saints should be outside their mothers' leading strings, and, like St. Theresa (of Avila!), be able to run a convent and dance every day before the Lord, and have visions and ecstasies, but also a fine, firm, human and tough point of standing (if I make myself clear!)— well, we can't have everything, and Marianne's decadence has been channelled off into her life and her prose, leaving the poetry pretty firm and pure and clear.

Yes; that is true. So I give my first, second and third choices to Marianne Moore! (Of the others, Stevens, as you say, has stopped, and become an affected old fool. Léonie has stopped, actually. I do think Harriet would want someone who has gone on, fought through, endured. Don't you?) (19 April 1944, 236)

Bogan refers to Moore's virginal life (Moore never married and lived with her mother) and to the effect of this life on the art. But Bogan, a survivor, was always one to give great credit to women who survived and carried on. *And* she thinks that Moore is heads taller than any of the male poets under consideration. Marianne Moore got the award.

Bogan continued to review the *Trilogy*. In 1945 she wrote a terse notice about H.D.'s second volume, *Tribute to the Angels:*

This American poet, for years resident in England, again affirms, in her clipped and polished style, her faith in a future rising from the ruins. Rather less mysticism than in the last year's *The Walls Do Not Fall.*[32]

Sarcasm here, in a clipped and polished style, with very little sympathy for the work. As I showed earlier, Bogan thought Civilization was a male subject. Moreover, a woman who had been raised a Catholic and now felt one had to live without philosophy, had no patience with this kind of "mysticism." Bogan dismissed *The Flowering of the Rod* (1946) with another short note:

H.D.'s mysticism, once implicit in her Imagist poems dealing with Greek symbols, is rather thin and shrill in this collection of her later works, what with their Biblical background and their redemption-by-suffering theme.[33]

I do not want to suggest that Bogan had to like H.D.'s poetry because it was written by a woman; what I am arguing is that her strict definitions of what a woman poet could do, and what she must not do, made it inevitable that she would have to dismiss many poets. She had her own standards for male poets as well, but I would argue that she allowed them greater range and diversity. As she wrote these reviews, she was comparing herself to other women poets.

Bogan's criticism in the fifties became both a passionate expression of the gift of women's poetry and thus implicitly a defense of her own work. She would keep asserting the view of the unique contribution of women. She undertook the large labor of a history, *Achievement in American Poetry, 1900–1950.* In the third chapter, "The Line of Truth and the Line of Feeling," she chronicles the career of Edwin Arlington Robinson and then turns to the contribution of women poets at the end of the nineteenth century:

It is clear that Robinson, in spite of his central contribution to poetic truth, did little to reconstitute any revivifying warmth of feeling in the poetry of his time. This task, it is now evident, was accomplished almost entirely by women poets through methods which proved to be as strong as they seemed to be delicate. The whole involved question of woman as artist cannot be dealt with here. We can at this point only follow the facts, as they unfold from the later years of the nineteenth century to the beginning of the twentieth; these facts prove that the line of poetic intensity which wavers and fades out and often completely fails in poetry written by men, on the feminine side moves on unbroken. Women, as 'intuitive' beings, are less open to the success and failures, the doubts and despair which attack reason's mechanisms. Women's feeling, at best, is closely attached to the organic heart of life . . . (AA 22–23)

Skillfully, Bogan elides over the problem of the woman artist—and moves quickly to her rhetorical purpose, the "facts," as she invokes her idea of the absolute complementarity, and difference, of women and men. Here she means "reason" in a philosophical sense, associating it with meditations on male civilization and existence. Her point is highly debatable: she is simplifying in order to make an argument. For in 1951 Bogan seemed particularly intent on establishing the idea of a viable female tradition. She goes on to acknowledge some of the damages of the sentimental aspects of the female tradition but asserts that real talent did emerge nonetheless, praising the work of Lizette Woodworth Reese, Louise Imogen Guiney, and Emily Dickinson. "Freshness and sincerity of emotion, and economical directness of method were . . . early apparent in formal poetry written by women well before the turn of the century" (AA 26). With these remarks, she is preparing the way for one of the basic ideas of her history of American poetry, the theme she had uncovered in writing "The Heart and the Lyre." Thus, in the chapter entitled "Postwar Achievement," the reader is not surprised to find that

In view of the confusion attendant upon the introduction and development, in the space of a few years, of such differing and explosive stylistic elements, it is remarkable that any reinforcement of the line of feeling was able to take place. This reinforcement was again chiefly due to a feminine vein of lyricism—a vein now reinvigorated by the addition of intellectual qualities. (AA 78)

The poetry establishment dominated by men has let experiments in form take over and again, the balance must be righted. Women are able to bring about this balance because they have "added" intellectual qualities to their work. Striking again is Bogan's internalization of the idea that women are not "naturally" given to activities of the mind; however, this is a quality we can acquire. Because women poets have learned to temper their feeling with intellect, they have achieved a balance that many male poets do not possess. Bogan then goes on to evaluate the poetry of Sara Teasdale, Edna St. Vincent Millay, Elinor Wylie, and Léonie Adams. Bogan had read Teasdale early in her career and continued to admire her; Teasdale also liked Bogan's poetry.[34] Of Teasdale, she writes that her work "had begun to free itself, in the twenties, from nearly all traces of a romantic vocabulary and a romantic tone" and thus she had achieved maturity:

> Miss Teasdale's lyrics . . . became increasingly lucid and tragic with the passage
> of time. She expressed not only the simplicities of traditional female feeling, but
> new subtleties of emotional nuance, and her last book, *Strange Victory*, pub-
> lished posthumously in 1933, shows classic depth and balance. (78–79)

The same kind of tension between feeling and structure was resolved in Elinor
Wylie's poetry:

> The gifts of Elinor Wylie (1885–1928) brought to the feminine lyric a mature
> emotional richness, as well as an added brilliance of craftsmanship. Mrs. Wylie
> early caught the note of Eliot's shorter poems. *Nets to Catch the Wind* (1921)
> revealed, as well, a firsthand apprenticeship to Donne, Herbert and Marvell. For
> a time she seemed overwhelmed by her own virtuosity; but she became more
> tellingly controlled as time went on, and in her last volume achieved a power
> that was directly structural. Although an undertone of rather inflated romanti-
> cism was constantly in evidence, her work as a whole was far more complex than
> that of any feminine predecessor. (AA 80)

This kind of critical evaluation at once reflects the modernist aesthetic and
looks back upon Rufus Griswold's observation, which Bogan had liked so
much, about the dangers of women's exuberant feeling. A true inheritor of the
Western tradition, Bogan in her early poetry had been obsessed with the
body/mind split; here, the dichotomy is cast in terms of man/woman, intellect/
emotion.[35] Yet Bogan was putting women into the tradition. Her little anthology at the end of *Achievement in American Poetry* includes more titles by
women than the usual groupings of selected American poems: Of twenty-one
poets, eleven are women.

In 1959 Louise Bogan published a review of women poets entitled, "In
Balance." She used the occasion to suggest that women poets have brought
emotion and form into equilibrium. And she wonders whether women are thus
in the process of creating a separate and distinctive poetic tradition:

> Is it possible, at the moment, to separate poetry written by women from
> poetry written by men, or has women's poetry been so thoroughly absorbed into
> the poetic situation at large that to set it apart must seem nearsighted and
> time-wasting? (PA 429)

At the height of her career, Bogan had resented being reviewed along with
other women poets. Now she points out that women had long ago abandoned
the sentimental tradition and that in the present age as "masculine poetic talent
has either tended to flatten into formalism or come to depend on shock tactics
of one kind or another, poetry written by women has gone its own way and
produced its own distinct lines of development" (430). Bogan's idea of a
distinct tradition is based on the great variety in women's poetry in the late

fifties: There are more women writing, there are many different kinds of writers. Yet it is primarily their departure from contemporary male poetic practice that defines this separate tradition. Her review goes on to praise most of the women whose publications had occasioned this review (Babette Deutsch, Ruth Stone, Barbara Howes, Marianne Moore) but takes a stand, once more, against modern mannerism and surrealism (in the work of one Katherine Hospkins), poetic modes not suited, or so Bogan believed, to feminine talent.

In September 1962 Bogan began work on a talk on women poets commissioned by Bennington College. She soon decided she was bored with the subject of "women bards" (JAR 133). So she began some more general research and her talk finally delved into women's history. For background, she read a witty, erudite (and now dated) book called *Women in Antiquity* by Charles Seltman, published in 1956. The lapsed Catholic in Bogan was moved by Seltman's characterization of the misogny of Paul and its impact upon the Church.[36] ("We hear the full denunciatory male voice sounding in passage after passage of the Old Testament; and we come upon the ancient concepts of Yin and Yang . . . we seem to come upon not only the harsh terms of a patriarchy, but of a matriarchy reversed, denied and denigrated . . ." (JAR 140–41). She finds herself interested in those eras that, according to her study, appear to be the most repressive for women, and she singles out the Victorian period. After her quick survey of women's history, Bogan turns to literature and the prose achievements of Dorothy Richardson and Virginia Woolf, favoring Richardson, with whom she more strongly identifies because she is from the working class.[37] Bogan always tempers her basic dislike of Woolf with some praise; in this essay, her negative point is that Woolf is an example of "extreme feminism," by which she means "the claim that absolute domination has existed, in an unbroken line, since the dawn of time" (JAR 141). Bogan thought that in *Three Guineas* Woolf inaccurately blamed male conspiracies for female subordination (". . . the insistence on masculine dominance has become obsessive, and the protesting voice shrill" [150]). Unlike Woolf, Bogan does not recognize the universal subordination of women but sees history as a record of the ebb and flow of women's fortunes, as she focuses on momentary female victories that she thinks derive from female nature, such as the spirituality of Saint Teresa. Once she makes clear her disavowal of "extreme feminism," she is able to speak in favor of a certain kind of feminism:

The word feminism today conjures up rather unhappy and dowdy figures; the suffragette stands in most young people's minds, I find, as a sort of large, formidable virtuous virago. But it is a word which has its own honor and radiance; it was lived for, and sometimes died for, by members of several generations of disenfranchised individuals who, far from representing a persecuted minority, stood for one half of the human race. (JA 135)

Having espoused the right of women to vote (and with eloquence), Bogan takes on Simone de Beauvoir, who is in the "extreme feminist" category, both anti-male and "openly ambivalent" about women:

> . . . a faint suspicion arises in the mind of the reader that, even if women were free, Beauvoir considers them unable to conduct their lives with true wisdom and fortitude, or to enter into a true "brotherhood" with men. Her attitude becomes openly ambivalent, somewhere on, or around, her five hundred and sixtieth page. Women chatter; women are forever trying to converse, to adapt, to arrange, rather than to destroy and build anew; they prefer compromise and adjustment to revolution . . . the later pages of *The Second Sex* turn rapidly from the comparatively cool and detached exposition . . . into a series of bitter diatribes against the modern "creative" woman. . . . In spite of all her protestations to the contrary, we feel, as we come to the end of this extraordinary work, that Mlle. de Beauvoir cherishes, in the deep recesses of her existentially trained self, a dislike, even a contempt, for the enigmatic, the intuitive, the graceful, the tender, the opalescent, the mercurial side of women's nature—the side that truly complements the virtues of the male. . . . (JA 151–53)

Contemporary feminist analyses of de Beauvoir, while praising her achievement, have also acknowledged her ambivalence toward most women and her identification with exceptional women and with men. Bogan gets to this point in her own way by poking fun at de Beauvoir's existential reasoning and invoking once again her belief in woman's basic nature. She is extremely hard on the book and uses it to illustrate her point about the excesses of feminism and of the special and different nature of women. We are sometimes able to recognize the sentiments of others because they are ours as well: Bogan understands de Beauvoir's ambivalence about women because she shares it.

Bogan's Bennington lecture ended with a summary of her views on women writers, drawn from the studies she made over the years, and which we have discussed, as well as an assertion of the complementarity of women and men and of the agency of women:

> The blows dealt women by social and religious change were real, and in certain times and places definitely maiming. But the articulate woman has always made it clear that she recognizes those biological and psychic laws which make her, as a modern eclectic analyst has recently pointed out, not the opposite or the "equal" (or the rival) of man, but man's complement.
>
> Women still have within them the memory of the distaff and the loom—and, we must remember, the memory of the dark, cruel, wanton goddesses. But because woman rarely has gone over, in the past, to a general and sustained low complicity or compliance in relation to her companion, man, we can hope for her future.
>
> And she listens, when a truly sibylline utterance falls from a sister's lips, such as the remark of the late Karen Blixen (surely one of the great writers of our or any other time) when she said: "Men and women are two locked caskets, of which each contains the key to the other." She listens to these words, with their ring of mysterious truth, with awe—not terror.

A close reader of Bogan cannot help but think of the casket imagery of a poem from her juvenilia which we shall discuss, "The Betrothal of King Cophetua," or notice the double-entendre of love and death suggested by "two locked caskets." We are at the same time reminded of the dramatic close of "The Heart and the Lyre," where Bogan described "the hungry eyes of the treasure hunter" looking for the lost fragments of a woman poet's song, that "destroyed jewel." Most striking, perhaps, is the reference, the only one in Bogan's criticism, to a woman writer as a "sister."

In 1963 Bogan published a review of the poetry of May Swenson and Anne Sexton with the startling title, "No Poetesses Maudites." Bogan begins by taking up again the theme which had first surfaced in her criticism in the forties—the corruption of male verse and the variety of the female line:

> Now that the work of male poets writing in English seems to have settled down into a few standard categories of material (bland, horrific) and of treatment (formal, loose), it is interesting to notice that poetry written by women (once thought to be limited to a rather narrow vein of personal lyricism) has also sorted itself out into a few basic kinds. (PA 431)

The review is more reminiscent of the sarcastic tone of the letters than of the bulk of the judicious criticism; at the age of sixty-six, only two years away from her joyous resignation from the *New Yorker,* Bogan seemed to be letting go. She then tells us what her generation thought feminism was all about: "To separate the work of women writers from the work of men, is, naturally, a highly unfeminist action" (431–32). (Interestingly, this is what Bogan was constantly doing and refusing to do.) True, to be feminist according to some definitions is to imitate men; another group of contemporary feminists are interested in separating the work of women from the work of men in order to show how ours is a different (though not necessarily superior) tradition. In this view difference is a result of culture, not nature. Bogan suggests the existence of a distinct tradition based on nature:

> But beneath surface likenesses, women's poetry continues to be unlike men's, all feminist statements to the contrary notwithstanding. Women function differently, in art as in life, and it should be an enlivening rather than a dismal fact that there are some things they either cannot or are unwilling to do, and others that they do very badly. (432)

This idea of the basic difference (and thus the complementarity) between women and men is one that feminists find limiting in the present age, arguing that biology and role should not be synonymous.

Bogan goes on to point out again how women, freeing themselves from male forms to which they were unsuited, created new traditions; and she writes a new version of her catalogue of styles and attitudes inappropriate to women writers. ("There are no poetesses maudites and there are no authentic women

Surrealists.") She praises May Swenson, whom she sees as an inheritor of Marianne Moore. ("Keeping themselves out of it, they display a woman's talent for dealing intensely and imaginatively with the concrete.") "Poetesses Maudites" ends with an appraisal of the work of Anne Sexton who, we would expect, would be at the farthest remove from what Louise Bogan could tolerate in poetry. In her letters, Bogan is frank and funny about Sexton. In 1969 she wrote to Ruth Limmer, "I have read a lot of tripe, and can't seem to get going on the NYer piece. I have decided, however, to mention the fact (at least) that Anne Sexton is the first woman in history to have written a hymn to her uterus . . ." (27 April 1969, 379). And of the two who are always paired, Sexton and Sylvia Plath, she exclaimed, "O why can't I write psychotic verse! Neurotic verse pales into insignificance beside what those—Sexton and Plath—can (could) turn out" (19 Sept. 1966, 369). Obviously, she felt this kind of poetry could get out of control. Her public appraisal of Sexton, while it notes the problems of her method and her subject, is generous:

> Anne Sexton, in her second book, *All My Pretty Ones,* as in her first, *To Bedlam and Back,* does take risks. She assumes the difficult and dangerous task of putting down the primary horrors of life, along with a good many of those secondary horrors which the imagination is able and willing to conjure up. Her realism deals with so many shocking secrets that her moderate use of Surrealistic language and method hardly counts; and these are almost always women's secrets that do not, in the ordinary way of things, get told. (PA 433)

No one knew better than Bogan both the primary and the secondary horrors; she registered these horrors through indirection. Her focus on secrets that do not usually get told is poignant because she, Bogan, stopped telling them relatively early. We are not surprised to hear that she feels that Sexton's confessional methods, on the other hand, are potentially dangerous:

> To outline personal relationships (and Mrs. Sexton's poems, unlike Miss Swenson's, are full of people) always at a high pitch of emotion requires courage; to describe fully the dark conflicts of the self without slipping over into the shrill voice of confession or the sobbing note of self-pity requires high control at every conscious and unconscious level. Mrs. Sexton sometimes crosses a boundary retrogressively—from large grief into small grievance, from natural fears to contrived ones. But she usually writes from the center of feminine experience, with the direct and open feeling that women, always vulnerable, have been shy of expressing in recent years. (PA 433)

With the last, we are immediately reminded of the admonition of "The Heart and the Lyre," written fifteen years before—that women poets had to give back to the world "its lost heart." The evaluation of Anne Sexton must be seen in the larger context of Bogan's criticism of women poets over the years; I think she consciously developed this perspective. Her public appraisal is more generous than her private views, as the letters to Ruth Limmer would indicate;

for, as we have seen, the confessional voice, the self-pity, were aspects of the female sensibility that Bogan thought should be suppressed. And, as we shall see, she excised her own "mawkish" poems. Yet she is willing to momentarily forget her point about female sentimentality in order to make another one that had become central for her since "The Heart and the Lyre"—the assertion of women's special role of bringing feeling, and thus balance, to poetry. Amy Lowell, too, had found her sisters strange and, at the same time, in the same poem, she had admitted ". . . I go dreaming on, / In love with these my spiritual relations."[38] The tales of ambivalence stretch through the centuries.

This, then, was the complex setting for Louise Bogan's poetry: a modernist milieu that had no great expectations for the work of women; subtle relationships among women poets, sometimes rivalrous, sometimes supportive; a powerful post as a critic, which led Bogan to think and write about the relationship of poetry by women to past and present traditions; her own experience of poetry and life, coupled with a shift in poetic taste in the forties, which in turn prompted a passionate defense of the gift of women's "heart" to poetry. In the next chapter, we will consider the poetic achievement that arose out of this skillful negotiation between her own particular talent and the female and male traditions of poetry.

Part II

The Achievement

> . . . only 16 poems published in the last
> year . . . I haven't worked at all. . . . Ten
> years from my successful *Seventeen* publica-
> tion, and a cold voice says: What have you
> done? . . . see that I have studied, thought
> and somehow not done anything more than
> teach a year: my mind lies fallow.
>
> —Sylvia Plath

> What compatibility can there be between the
> creed offering hope of a way of speaking
> beyond the ordinary, touching perfection, a
> complex perfection associable with nothing
> less complex than truth, and the craft tying
> the hope to verbal rituals. . . . If poets
> strain hard enough they must reach the
> crisis-point at which division between creed
> and craft reveals itself to be absolute . . . no
> poet before me has gone to the very break-
> ing point. . . . The last poems I wrote are
> contained in my *Collected Poems* published
> in 1938. I can be seen, in that book, to be
> striving to find at once the poetic extreme
> *and,* the mark of human fullness of
> utterance—and to be heading toward
> finalities of proof of poetry, and of the
> poet-role itself.
>
> —Laura Riding

IV.

"EPITAPH FOR A ROMANTIC WOMAN"

Early and Uncollected Poems

> Leaning, he took her face between his hands
> She turned her eyes to him, and did not
> speak.
>
> —"The Betrothal of King Cophetua"

> He has kissed me with closed eyes,
> Embraced me with a hidden face,
> And I did not know whose eyes he took
> and whose face burned behind his
> eyelids.
>
> —"The Young Wife"

> You have put your two hands upon me, and
> your mouth,
> You have said my name as a prayer.
>
> —"Betrothed"

Nothing could be more dangerous for a woman poet who wanted to establish herself as A Poet in the twenties than to publish an entire volume on the disillusionments of romantic love. Yet this is exactly what Louise Bogan did with her first book, *Body of This Death,* published in 1923 when she was twenty-six years old. As we have shown, Bogan believed that lyric poetry came out of experience; and the center of her experience in these years was her first love and marriage. In this section, I want to bring to light the editorial decisions Bogan made about her first book. She did not include all the poems she had written or even all those she had published in small magazines. These were the first stages of her prunings; later, she would cut some of the poems of the original edition of *Body of This Death* as subsequent collections were released. In fact, I do not disagree with most of Bogan's youthful artistic decisions, for they have yielded a commanding first volume. Our survey of these early poems will show us something about the hard work that goes into being a poet and something about Bogan's developing clarity about what she wanted her poetry to be, that is, her self-image as a poet, an image wrought both of individual and cultural identities.

Bogan's sense of poetry and experience came from literature. On the one hand, as Margaret Homans has perceptively pointed out, "biographical and thematic interpretations only partly illuminate" women's poetry for there is also "a different order of 'female experience'" which contributes "in a major way to the shaping of poetry by women: literary experience, the experience of reading poetry written almost exclusively by men." "Literary experience," she adds, "is the poet's equivalent to the novelist's societal experience."[1] Bogan's idea of poetry came from her reading, as I have shown; she also took her images of love from these readings. Thus, a study of the suppressed poems gives us insights into both Bogan's creation of her voice and her expectations for romantic love. Put another way, this exploration will help us to see the complex interrelationship between the artist and the woman. How did Louise Bogan's self-definition as an artist influence her conception of womanhood and how, in turn, did her image of femininity impinge on her artistic expression?

Louise Bogan's college poems are the first place to look for a clue to her beginnings as an artist and as a woman with notions of romantic love. "The Betrothal of King Cophetua" was published the year of her marriage. Jaqueline Ridgeway accurately cites Tennyson's "The Beggar Maid" as the model for this ornate college poem. ("Barefooted came the beggar maid / Before the king Cophetua.")[2] Bogan's poem gives us one perspective on the motivations of romantic love. In it, a king summons a young girl. Memory has inspired his love since she brings back to the king "old dreams / his youth knew." Here is a profound insight into romance among the middle-aged, a truth Bogan may have intuited from her involvement with an older man. Before him in the court the girl is anonymous, AnyGirl; she has no name and cannot remember where she is from. The king gives her a "casket," a little box full of jewels: Even so young a poet must have meant the double entendre of love and death in that image. Moreover, the jewel box stands blatantly for sexual awakening.

The Betrothal of King Cophetua

When they had brought her at the king's behest,
The courtyard dusk felt cool to her forehead's heat,
She silent stood, the sun on her bruised feet.
The evening shadow lay against her breast.

"Your name?" he asked.
"I have not any name."
Her round voice held the soul of windless streams
Fringed to the bank with grasses—of old dreams

His youth knew. His words broke, and he was mute,
Then asked again "You come from out what land?
   "I have forgotten."
   Under trees of fruit
He had seen her first as they bowed in the ripening year,
Fragrant her lips with fruit, and stained her hand.
He said "Come nearer," and she came more near.

A casket then he gave to her like flame
Beneath the lid, like flame into the dark
The jewels sprawled and looped and shot their spark
Star-wise: peridot, beryl, winy sard
And icy straps of diamond.

   Above,
Beyond where to the sky the roof cut hard
Called, notes like heavy water to a wave
Were falling, and with pain her heart knew love . . .
The box crashed, the heaped gems spilled to the pave.

Blindly, through the dark, to his side she came,
Her feet seemed shod with rain so swift they were.
Like wings on her forehead folded lay her hair,
And she was wild and sweet.
   "I am a king,"
He said, "But if I give you jewels, lands,
And you spurn all, I have no other thing,
No more to give, if it be not love you seek . . ."
Leaning, he took her face between his hands;
She turned her eyes to him, and did not speak.[3]

The poem is imitative, decorative, its point of view almost shocking when
one considers that its author was about to enter into marriage. It perfectly
captures what Rachel Blau DuPlessis has called "romantic thralldom":

> Romantic thralldom is an all-encompassing, totally defining love between
> unequals. The lover has the power of conferring self-worth and purpose upon
> the loved one. Such love is possessive, and while those enthralled feel it com-
> pletes and even transforms them, they are also enslaved. The eroticism of
> romantic love, born of this unequal relationship between the sexes, may depend
> for its satisfaction upon dominance and submission. Thralldom insists upon the
> differences between the sexes, encouraging a sense of mystery surrounding the
> motives and powers of the lover: thus it begins with and ends in sexual polariza-
> tion. Viewed from a critical, feminist perspective, the sense of completion or
> transformation that often accompanies thralldom in love has the high price of
> obliteration and paralysis, for the entranced self is entirely defined by another. I
> do not need to emphasize that this kind of love is socially learned and that it is
> central in our culture.[4]

"The Betrothal of King Cophetua" is not without its moments; its repeti-
tions and its pauses, its play with sound, and an evocation of stillness and
sensuality show a predilection for poetry. Moreover, the effect of immobility

Bogan achieves as she renders the girl's passivity and her silence is one she would perfect for *Body of This Death*. The association of love with pain—and women's masochistic pursuit of such relations—would stay in her poetry, reaching both its fullest expression and its release in *Dark Summer*.

Similar concerns of theme and style are evident in Bogan's first professional publication in 1917 in *Others*, when she was twenty years old. There she published "Betrothed," which she liked well enough to include in all subsequent collections through 1968, and a companion poem, "The Young Wife," which she would jettison. "The Young Wife" presents a veritable catalogue of women's disappointments, the feelings felt when romantic hopes are denied for the first time. Here is complete defeat and resignation and self-abnegation, here possessiveness and jealousy toward other women. But most striking, and certainly most relevant to the poet who must be a critic of her own work, is the poem's expression of a woman's passivity, self-pity, and utter powerlessness:

The Young Wife

I

I do not believe in this first happiness,
But one day I shall know that love is not a fruited bough
Low bending to the hand;
One day I shall know that love is the secret wind
Rippling the grass
Along hillsides in the night;
That it is the tree in spring
Holding lightly in the air its shining twigs
And with its roots throbbing in darkness.

So I shall take less love now
And not think it as due me,
And I shall not watch the eyes of my lover, their every glance,
Nor take his day as mine, nor count the hours of his night.
Even though love comes hard
With all the labor of the spring,
Though I may wish to grasp that for which I have suffered
And crush it to me with a tight hand.

A day comes when all must go.
Love does not stand;
Love does not wait;
No man can follow after love—
A day dawns with a wild sky,
I have laid my hand to the earth and felt how it is cold,
I have seen the little leaves that the poplar tree lets fall upon the wind.

II

Had I the sweet skin of Helen
and Deirdre's autumn-colored hair
I could not be as beautiful as all beautiful women.

I cannot have the voices of all beautiful women
Were my voice bright with the trill and quiver of water,—
Nor their laughter
Nor their speech.
Though I might choose delicate words
I could not speak so fair as they.

They have taken everything from me,
The beautiful women my lover has had before me,—
Gentle touches of cheek to cheek,
The embraces of passion and of terror;
They have given all to him before me:
Love in the night,
Tears,
Trust and suffering and long desire—
I can but repeat these, and say them over,
All love's thousand things.

He has kissed me with closed eyes,
Embraced me with a hidden face,
And I did not know whose kiss he took and whose face burned behind his eyelids.

And all women will bear me out in this,
All women now yielding to a lover,
And all of other years:
Ye, poor queens,
And ye, poor haughty ladies.[5]

"The Young Wife," with a title more explicit, more autobiographical, than would be usual in her oeuvre, is in fact two poems. In the first, there is the certainty, which would remain in Bogan's work and in her psyche, that love is doomed even as it begins; and there are those terrible youthful confusions about what love is (mystery? high? deep? phallic?). The imagery of the opening lines seems almost unconscious. The young woman's possessiveness is extreme and ultimately killing, when the desire to live depends on romantic love. This mood of resignation and self-pity, the sense of being *under* and consumed, is arrested for just one moment, with a line of bitter irony that brings a hint of poetry to come: "I have laid my hand to the earth and felt how it is cold." This is pure Bogan.

Part II of "The Young Wife" presents another version of the knowledge of the King Cophetua poem. Here, too, the man's love is made up of memory and dream, memories of the women he has known and fantasies of those in his future. There is frightening anonymity, a kind of death, in the love ritual of the next to last stanza, and as the epigraphs show, this is an effect that Bogan was working to achieve. The understanding of love's rituals performed in empty and unfeeling and unthinking repetition will bring the poet and the woman closer to a sense of love that is self-defined. However, the inexperienced young woman is fatalistic: Here again we have that self-fulfilling prophecy that romantic love is pain. "The Young Wife" is all grieving pathos, the voice of a half-child, half-woman. Stylistically and thematically, it is everything that

Bogan over the years would strenuously avoid: She wanted concise images, not narrative voice; strength, not self-pity; wisdom, not "immature" emotion. Above all, she wanted some measure of *control* over her imagery and her romantic life.

For reasons at once obvious and obscure, Bogan continued to like the companion poem to "The Young Wife." "Betrothed," first published in 1917, is the earliest poem of the final collection, *The Blue Estuaries:*

Betrothed

> You have put your two hands upon me, and your mouth,
> You have said my name as a prayer.
> Here where trees are planted by the water
> I have watched your eyes, cleansed from regret,
> And your lips, closed over all that love cannot say.
>
> My mother remembers the agony of her womb
> And long years that seemed to promise more than this.
> She says, "You do not love me,
> You do not want me,
> You will go away."
>
> In the country whereto I go
> I shall not see the face of my friend
> Nor her hair the color of sunburnt grasses;
> Together, we shall not find
> The land on whose hills bends the new moon
> In air traversed of birds.
>
> What have I thought of love?
> I have said, "It is beauty and sorrow."
> I have thought it would bring me lost delights, and splendor
> As a wind out of old time. . . .
>
> But there is only the evening here
> And the sound of willows
> Now and again dipping their long oval leaves in the water.

(7)

In writing "Betrothed," Bogan perfected the use of ritual (a discovery of the King Cophetua poem) to suggest the social prescriptions of romantic love. She accomplishes this effect by freezing gesture within a few lines, thus underlining love's static qualities. Mouth, hands, eyes (in the selections of the epigraph) are stilled, so that we feel death—not bounteous dynamic life.

What is most curious about "Betrothed" is the placement at poem's center of two women the narrator will leave in order to marry—her mother and a woman friend. These stanzas do not work artistically because the poet has not been successful in connecting them to the rest of the poem. Yet in them there is a subtle, even unconscious recognition of a basic female reality: When we choose heterosexual love, we often leave behind those female attachments that had been sustaining (if conflicted) in our younger years. The second stanza refers quite directly to her mother's opposition to her marriage. Ruth Limmer says that, "Her mother was opposed, she told me once; she threatened, had a heart attack. 'But I was trying to escape.' Instead of going on to Radcliffe, where she had been offered a scholarship after one year at Boston University, Bogan defied her mother and married" (JAR xxii). In the third stanza, the speaker tenderly evokes this woman friend she will leave behind.

The penultimate stanza of "Betrothed" is deeply romantic in feeling and language in a way that surprisingly survived Bogan's censorious eye; the theme of beauty and sorrow is a direct quotation from the whole body of romantic poetry. Feminist critics have written eloquently about how women's ideas of romantic love are formed by fiction.[6] Bogan's imagination, as we have said, was fired by poetry: From male poets, she derived some of her fantasies, and some of her expressions, of romantic love. In the final stanza, the young poet tests an increasing ability to convey sadness and stillness through delicate observations of nature. I think Bogan continued to like this poem in part because of memory, this time poetic memory: "Betrothed" has the same hush and delicacy as some of the nineteenth-century British poetry she read as a young girl and imitated as a high school poet, in a work such as "Night in Summer," with its tender opening quatrain:

> The restless sea before my window breaks
> All night beneath the stars that bend to see;
> Full of unrest, and sad, and longingly,
> It sings its soft, sad song as day awakes . . .[7]

It is not surprising that Bogan decided against "Survival," which she first published in the *Measure* in November 1921.

Survival

> I hoped that you would die out from me
> With the year.
> Between you and my heart I thrust
> The glittering seasons.
>
> I denied you with late summer,
> Watching the green-white hydrangea change
> To petalled balls of thin and ashen blue,
> And nasturtiums, hot orange on stems like ice or glass
> Shriveling by round leaves.
>
> I went on to autumn
> Without you,
> Seeing hills burdened by trees colored unevenly:
> Applered, pearyellow,
> And leaves falling in ravines, through bitter smoke,
> Falling indirectly,
> A long waver and turn.

Those evenings came
High and shining over rivers like quicksilver;
And latest autumn:
The underbrush sienna, cut, twisted, carved,
Red berries shaken through it like beads
Scattered in barbaric hair.

Nothing moves in the fields that once had the grass.
To look upon the fields
Is like silence laid upon the eyes.
The house is shut sternly
From limitless radiance outside
In these days of afternoon stars.
The year dies out.
Who are you to be stronger than the year?
I have you like long cold sunshine in an empty room,
Through and beyond black thaws that rot the snow.[8]

The piling up of adjectives and nouns in the second and third stanzas, inspired by her reading of the Pre-Raphaelites, prevents us from seeing and feeling. Toward the end of the third stanza and in the fourth, she begins to break through to a greater simplicity of expression. In fact, these lines are the inspiration for the "Medusa" poem (BE 4), which she would publish only a month later in the *New Republic*, bringing the feelings of stillness and dread in "Survival" to perfect realization. Having found compression in the third and fourth stanzas of "Survival," she is able in the last one to interiorize, both literally and figuratively. The line "I have you like long cold sunshine in an empty room" is masterly in its pace and power; she takes the risk, and succeeds, with a common adjective that serves her for bitterness and irony. The last line returns to a kind of thick description that prevents seeing. Predictably, Bogan would censor "Survival" for its Rossettian overtones, its explicit title and expression of revenge and self-pity, emotions she would decide did not belong in poetry. For us, "Survival" is a powerful example of just how hard Louise Bogan worked to become a modernist poet.

Of five poems published in *Poetry* in August 1922 under the title "Beginning and End," only one, "Knowledge," survived Bogan's prunings. She would abandon "Elders," "Resolve," "Leave-taking," and "To a Dead Lover" as she selected poems for *Body of This Death*. In "Elders," she so overloads the second stanza that again we cannot visualize or feel her point; nonetheless, the irony she would become famous for breaks through as berries "Ripe for the mouths of chance lovers, / Or birds."[9] "Resolve," "Leave-taking," and "To a Dead Lover" find her still immersed in the experience; "Knowledge" (BE 9) fits her conception of art because it is a more distant, almost abstract summary of the whole devastating experience of disillusioned love. In contrast, it is likely that Bogan found the emotions expressed in "Resolve" too childish:

Resolve

So that I shall no longer tarnish with my fingers
The bright steel of your power,
I shall be hardened against you,
A shield tightened upon its rim.

A stern oval to be pierced by no weapon,
Metal stretched and shaped against you.
For a long time I shall go
Spanned by the round of my strength.

Changeless, in spite of change,
My resolve undefeated;
Though now I see the evening moon, soon to wane,
Stand clearly and alone in the early dark,
Above the stirring spindles of the leaves.[10]

The tone is petulant, the resolve ineffectual because the woman speaks out of utter powerlessness. The childish tone contrasts with the poem's battle imagery, which suggests an opposition of female (oval) and male (weapon). Defiance carved out of strength would emerge at the end of *Body of This Death*, though the solution suggested here, removal, chastity, is also a dominant theme of the first book. In the last, moving stanza, a moment of silence, and a great sense of loss, are conveyed through light and dark trees, set against steely resolve: again, the imagery, probably quite unconsciously, evokes female and male.

This same self-destructive resolve is present in a poem by Sara Teasdale that appeared in *Rivers to the Sea* in 1915. Bogan never cited Teasdale as one of her "influences," yet this is the very poem she chose as the Teasdale selection for her anthology of American poetry at the end of *Achievement in American Poetry, 1900–1950* (1951). There are echoes of Teasdale in many of Louise Bogan's early poems:

Sara Teasdale (1884–1933)

When I am dead and over me bright April
    Shakes out her rain-drenched hair,
Tho' you should lean above me broken-hearted,
    I shall not care.

I shall have peace, as leafy trees are peaceful
    When rain bends down the bough,
And I shall be more silent and cold-hearted
    Than you are now.

Bogan's anthology does not give the poem's title: "I Shall Not Care."[11]

The sense of utter defeat is repeated in "Leave-taking," even as the poet comes out of the experience long enough to recognize the destructiveness of the relationship for both woman and man. For love has been a form of death:

Leave-taking

I do not know where either of us can turn
Just at first, waking from the sleep of each other.
I do not know how we can bear
The river struck by the gold plummet of the moon,
Or many trees shaken together in the darkness.
We shall wish not to be alone
And that love were not dispersed and set free—
Though you defeat me,
And I be heavy upon you.

But like earth heaped over the heart
Is love grown perfect.
Like a shell over the beat of life
Is love perfect to the last.
So let it be the same
Whether we turn to the dark or to the kiss of another;
Let us know this for leave-taking,
That I may not be heavy upon you,
That you may blind me no more.[12]

Bogan's irony and distancing enter successfully here with her invocation of "perfect" love. From the romantic standpoint, perfect love is hermetic, self-contained, two people in relation only to each other and cut off from the social world. In "Leave-taking," there is a new theme suggesting that the woman's dependence, originally invited, has become too much for the man. Circular form is used again as metaphor for enclosure and a kind of death; here, "shell" serves as "oval" did in "Resolve." The poem is more successful than many of her earliest ones because of its matter-of-fact tone, which bears the weight of sadness and its acceptance of ending. Bogan would, nonetheless, abandon it in favor of "Words for Departure," which carries the same theme of the difficulty of leave-taking even when one sees its necessity.

"To a Dead Lover" is a title of double meaning; the poem was written after the death of love and the death in 1920 of the husband she had left the year before.

To a Dead Lover

The dark is thrown
Back from the brightness, like hair
Cast over a shoulder.
I am alone,
Four years older;
Like the chairs and the walls
Which I once watched brighten
With you beside me. I was to waken
Never like this, whatever came or was taken.

The stalk grows, the year beats on the wind.
Apples come, and the month for their fall.
The bark spreads, the roots tighten.

Though today be the last
Or tomorrow all,
You will not mind.

That I may not remember
Does not matter.
I shall not be with you again.
What we knew, even now
Must scatter
And be ruined, and blow
Like dust in the rain.

You have been dead a long season
And have less than desire
Who were lover with lover;
And I have life—that old reason
To wait for what comes
To leave what is over.[13]

I find this the most successful of the "Beginning and End" poems, as it practices that spareness and understatement that Bogan would use so successfully in *Body of This Death*. There is great intensity, an enormous sadness in this poem, conveyed through stripped language and simple declarative sentences. Love scattered and dispersed is here as it had been in "Leave-taking." The sense of silence and death, the irony—these she would bring with even greater power to her first book. By now it should be clear that the paradoxical idea that formed her 1923 volume—the body as site both of love and death—grew out of the writing of these earlier poems. Although she jettisoned these selections, they are valuable both for what they reveal about Bogan's development as a poet and for what they tell us about how a young woman feels after the first loss of belief in romantic love.

Suppressed Poems from *Body of This Death*

We all have to choose whatever subject-matter allows us the most powerful and most secret release; and that is a personal affair.

—T. S. Eliot

Five poems published in *Body of This Death* (1923) were not included in later collections. "Decoration," the second selection in the original edition, is an ornate pseudo-symbolist poem that deserves to be forgotten; for some reason, Louis Untermeyer kept putting it in his anthologies and this annoyed Bogan.[14] The excision of the following poem is more problematic:

Epitaph for a Romantic Woman

She has attained the permanence
She dreamed of, where old stones lie sunning.
Untended stalks blow over her
Even and swift, like young men running.

> Always in the heart she loved
> Others had lived,—she heard their laughter.
> She lies where none has lain before,
> Where certainly none will follow after.
>
> (BD 18)

Why did Bogan jettison this poem? Perhaps she felt the renunciation theme was evident enough in *Body of This Death* or perhaps she was again excising those feelings of jealousy first registered in "The Young Wife," who senses the presence of other women in her own love relationship. Perhaps she found the couplet that ends the first stanza too funny for a serious poem. (It is, a little, but strikingly vivid as well.) The poem's title is a gloss on the whole first volume; its bitterness is convincing, as is its delineation of the love that becomes death. These qualities—and the terrible irony of its last lines—make it, in my view, worth preserving.

Late in her career Bogan decided against another short lyric and two longer narrative poems. She used the old-fashioned adjective "mawkish" ("having a sweet, weak, sickening taste; insipid, sentimental") to describe her assessment of "Song" and "A Letter."[15]

This is a letter to her editor, John Hall Wheelock, as she made the choices for her first collection, *Poems and New Poems:*

> I find it easy to send back this proof quickly; there is nothing controversial in the choices.—I don't think, however, that we can keep "A Letter." There is something wrong with it; I can't say just what. Something sentimental or unfinished or mawkish. Whatever it is, I don't like it. So please let's take it out.—I don't like "Love me because I am lost," either. Don't you think we might dispense with that as well?
>
> It isn't that I'm turning on my early self. But the girl of 23 and 24, who wrote most of these early poems, was so seldom mawkish, that I want her not to be mawkish at all.—You understand, I am sure . . . So please do make excision marks in *both* instances; and let's get that choice off our minds. (28 July 1941, 222)

Bogan seems to be agonizing a bit over her choice. Here is the "Song" she excised:

> Song
>
> Love me because I am lost;
> Love me that I am undone.
> That is brave,—no man has wished it,
> Not one.
>
> Be strong, to look on my heart
> As others look on my face.
> Love me,—I tell you that it is a ravaged
> Terrible place.
>
> (BD 25)

Surely the forty-four-year-old, accomplished, respected poet did not want to be seen this way. There are echoes of the female tradition in "Song," that "poor me" tone she associated with the nineteenth century. Self-pity is an emotion male poets allow themselves; but a woman conscious of the female tradition may decide she has to excise such feeling. To be an artist is to have the right to edit out aspects of character that seem unattractive. For Bogan, the poem is too confessional, too revealing of a weak moment, even if it is acutely insightful about the response to disappointed love by a woman who feels powerless. She did not want this kind of emotion in her work; rather, irony and backbone must structure her poems.

"A Letter" expresses as much pain as "Song" but in a form rare in Bogan's oeuvre. This is a long narrative poem which renders a woman in despair.

A Letter

I came here, being stricken, stumbling out
At last from streets; the sun, decreasing, took me
For days, the time being the last of autumn,
The thickets not yet stark, but quivering
With tiny colors, like some brush strokes in
The manner of the pointillists; small yellows
Dart shaped, little reds in different pattern,
Clicks and notches of color on threaded bushes,
A cracked and fluent heaven, and a brown earth.
I had these, and my food and sleep—enough.

This is a countryside of roofless houses,—
Taverns to rain,—doorsteps of millstones, lintels
Leaning and delicate, foundations sprung to lilacs,
Orchards where boughs like roots strike into the sky.
Here I could well devise the journey to nothing,
At night getting down from the wagon by the black barns,
The zenith a point of darkness, breaking to bits,
Showering motionless stars over the houses.
Scenes relentless—the black and white grooves of a woodcut.

But why the journey to nothing or any desire?
Why the heart taken by even senseless adventure,
The goal a coffer of dust? Give my mouth to the air,
Let arrogant pain lick my flesh with a tongue
Rough as a cat's; remember the smell of cold mornings,
The dried beauty of women, the exquisite skin
Under the chins of young girls, young men's rough beards,—
The cringing promise of this one, that one's apology
For the knife struck down to the bone, gladioli in sick rooms,
Asters and dahlias, flowers like ruches, rosettes . . .

Forever enough to part grass over the stones
By some brook or well, the lovely seed-shedding stalks;
To hear in the single wind diverse branches
Repeating their sounds to the sky—that sky like scaled mackerel,

Fleeing the fields—to be defended from silence,
To feel my body as arid, as safe as a twig
Broken away from whatever growth could spare it
Up to a spring, or hold it softly in summer
Or beat it under in snow.

                                           I must get well.
Walk on strong legs, leap the hurdles of sense,
Reason again, come back to my old patchwork logic,
Addition, subtraction, money, clothes, clocks,
Memories (freesias, smelling slightly of snow and of flesh
In a room with blue curtains) ambition, despair.
I must feel again who had given feeling over,
Challenge laughter, take tears, play the piano,
Form judgments, blame a crude world for disaster.

To escape is nothing. Not to escape is nothing.
The farmer's wife stands with a halo of darkness
Rounding her head. Water drips in the kitchen
Tapping the sink. To-day the maples have split
Limb from the trunk with the ice, a fresh wooden wound.
The vines are distorted with ice, ice burdens the breaking
Roofs I have told you of.

                            Shall I play the pavanne
For a dead child or the scene where that girl
Lets fall her hair, and the loud chords descend
As though her hair were metal, clashing along
Over the tower, and a dumb chord receives it?
This may be wisdom: abstinence, beauty is nothing,
That you regret me, that I feign defiance.
And now I have written you this, it is nothing.

                                              (BD 5–7)

"A Letter" chronicles a despair that borders on madness: It is written to a former lover and placed in a volume of poems, *Body of This Death*, devoted to the disillusionments of love. Time moves from autumn to winter in a setting that supplies a metaphor for the estranged state of the soul. Under such conditions of emotional exhaustion, there is an attempt to be satisfied with simple survival ("I had these, and my food and sleep—enough.") The slow, careful description in the first and second stanzas is the woman's attempt to come to terms with this strange land where she "could well devise the journey to nothing," where "scenes relentless" mirror the negations of the heart. In the third stanza, however, despair gives way to defiance and a powerful urge to feel the pain; there is as well a bitterness that threatens to turn into a hatred of life. The sound of the poem changes with the fourth stanza, whose modulations and "s" sounds are interrupted by a startling simile, "A sky like scaled mackerel." In the northeast, a mackerel sky is a portent of rain; water tries to enter this passage but the body would steal itself away from the pain of life and love. "To feel my body as arid, as safe as a twig . . ." is reminiscent of the dryness, and the death wish, of "Men Loved Wholly Beyond Wisdom" in the same volume:

> What a marvel to be wise,
> To love never in this manner.
> To be quiet in the fern
> Like a thing gone dead and still,
> Listening to the prisoned cricket
> Shake its terrible, dissembling
> Music in the granite hill.
>
> (16)

This poem, which scores the tendency of women to love too much, is one Bogan liked for its economy of expression. She always chose the condensed lyric over the more revealing, long-lined poems like "A Letter" even if, as in the fifth stanza, they were extraordinarily moving: To put off insanity, the woman names everyday things ("money, clothes, clocks") as though she were trying to call the mundane back into reality. This coming to terms with living occurs slowly, bravely. To "blame a crude world for disaster" is a rare concession from Bogan who proudly took responsibility for all her difficulties. But is it not sometimes necessary to admit that events conspire against us?

The opposites of the sixth stanza ("To escape is nothing. Not to escape is nothing.") show despair's results: a sense of the sameness of all things, a lack of distinctions, and a belief that nothing matters. Bogan would put this nihilistic sentiment and this syntax to good use in *Body of This Death:*

In the dead scene of "Medusa,"

> The water will always fall, and will not fall . . .
>
> (4)

For the woman of "The Crows,"

> The heart's laughter will be to her
> The crying of the crows,
>
> Who slide in the air with the same voice
> Over what yields not, and what yields . . .
>
> (17)

and in "The Changed Woman,"

> The wound heals over, and is set
> In the whole flesh, and is not much
> Quite to remember or forget.
>
> (22)

In the sixth stanza there is a change of season, bringing a setting reminiscent of "The Flume," another suppressed narrative poem that uses the sound of water as metaphor for inner torment; monotony, dread, destruction, are evoked in these lines, which finally break through, in the final stanza, to lament and the question, "What shall I do with this grief?", posed with reference to Debussy's *Pélleas and Mélisande.* This allusion to that story of innocent and tragic youthful love does raise the pitch of the poem to perhaps a too dramatic degree. (The opera had been one of Bogan's favorites as a young girl and she had played parts of it on the piano many times.)[16] This hyperbolic moment is quickly undercut by the speaker's reassertion of the "nothingness" of her feelings and her expression of them, an assertion the very existence of the poem denies.

"Sentimental, unfinished, mawkish"—this is Bogan's judgment of a poem I find evocative of the wildness of despair and the attempt to pull oneself from the brink. In fact, the poem succeeds in the way that one of Bogan's favorite novelists succeeds: "The book (*Follow Thy Fair Sun* by Viola Meynell) is the most remarkable study of the agony of love that I have ever read, and despair is traced, as is usually not the case, with the author's bare nerves and sensibilities. It is not wrapped up in literature; it occurs on the page before us, as in the best drama and poetry. Colette is the only other woman I know who has looked so closely and felt so accurately that her words have the value of some major discovery about life" (To John Hall Wheelock, 29 Oct. 1935, 114).

I think "A Letter" has a similar power. But it is not a measured lyric, and it is too self-revealing, and perhaps even for Bogan, too despairing. My assumption in this discussion is that there is something valuable about these records of human emotion, be they poems or novels. Now, there has been much discussion among feminist theorists of poetry about whether one can take a poem to be true, that is reflective of the poet's experience. Margaret Homans has taken the point of view that, since language is "inherently fictive," we cannot make an assumption of relationship between truth or autobiography and the poem.[17] Carolyn Burke, in an article in *Feminist Studies,* links her work on the "experimental" female modernists with Homans's theoretical perspective; Mina Loy, Gertrude Stein, and Marianne Moore write in "more impersonal or nonpersonal voices," attached as they were to a "new vision of subjectivity" that leaves off ideas of the self developed by ego psychology.[18] Cheryl Walker, writing of the nineteenth-century female tradition, and responding to Homans's formulation, says these poets "wanted their poems to convey autobiographical messages and these messages, for all that they come veiled and "slant," are part of these poets' aims."[19] It is clear that this argument depends on which poet one is discussing. Bogan's aesthetic depended on the expression of emotion based in experience; and such a stated aesthetic leads us to an interpretation that includes a large measure of autobiography and the expectation that there is some "truth" in the poetry, some truth for Bogan herself and something of the "truth" of women.

Many of the themes of *Body of This Death* are sounded in "A Letter": devastating disillusionment in romantic love, a sense of loss and confusion that leads to the edge of madness, a desire for death. In the original version of *Body of This Death,* "Words for Departure" is placed between "Betrothed," marking the melancholy of a marriage, and "Ad Castitatem," yet another defiant pledge of chastity. The poem's first stanza again uses the imagery of negation:

Words for Departure

Nothing was remembered, nothing forgotten.
When we awoke, wagons were passing on the warm summer pavements,
The window-sills were wet from rain in the night,
Birds scattered and settled over chimneypots
As among grotesque trees.

Nothing was accepted, nothing looked beyond.
Slight-voiced bells separated hour from hour,
The afternoon sifted coolness
And people drew together in streets becoming deserted.
There was a moon, and light in a shop-front,
And dusk falling like precipitous water.

Hand clasped hand,
Forehead still bowed to forehead—
Nothing was lost, nothing possessed,
There was no gift nor denial.

Lovers awake, having accepted the end of an affair, seemingly without bitterness and accusation. In the second stanza, the speaker remembers the liaison in
its full blossoming:

I have remembered you.
You were not the town visited once,
Nor the road falling behind running feet.

You were awkward as flesh
And lighter than frost or ashes.

You were the rind,
And the white-juiced apple,
The song, and the words waiting for music.

In the third stanza, she sends her lover off to a new companion with some
advice:

You have learned the beginning;
Go from mine to the other.

Be together; eat, dance, despair,
Sleep, be threatened, endure.
You will know the way of that.

But at the end, be insolent;
Be absurd—strike the thing short off;
Be mad—only do not let talk
Wear the bloom from silence.

And go away without fire or lantern.
Let there be some uncertainty about your departure.

(BD 10)

"Words of Departure" has a strong emotional impact precisely because it is direct and immediate; we feel the movement of emotion through the stages of an experience. Bogan was not comfortable with free verse modes so it is not surprising she struck this poem; Elizabeth Frank says she also "kept the poem out of her collected editions, feeling its ending was too dependent on a fashionable and utterly insincere 'Greenwich Village' attitude of toleration toward sexual rivals."[20] I find the bravado unconvincing but all the more poignant because it is a pose. The moods of the poem—from a moment of pleasure to memory to a "keep your chin up" attitude—are vividly reflective of experience and satisfying as art.

This excursion has unburied some poems by Louise Bogan that deserve to be read as they bring insight into her developing self-image as a modern woman poet. Let us turn now to the first volume of poems as the poet chose to present it to us in her final collection, *The Blue Estuaries*.

Body of This Death (1923)

What was it that you sought?
I sought love. Having been taught by memory and example.

—JAR 56

Body of This Death (1923) is Louise Bogan's most immediate volume. It is one of the most stunning poetic records in English of a young woman's response to the first failure of love. In its subject matter, the book belongs to the female tradition; in its intense, stripped expression of the devastations of romantic love, it leans toward modernist formalism. This first volume of poems, published in 1923 when Bogan was twenty-six, registers a whole range of responses to a monumental disappointment: It records complete, paralyzed devastation; the sudden plunge into a devotion to chastity; forms of self-pity that, on closer examination, look more like a desperate response to feelings of entrapment and defiance, in which elements both of power and powerlessness lie.

The title of the book comes out of the poet's Catholic upbringing: the body, seat of pleasure, is also the repository of death. More precisely, St. Paul, from whom Bogan took the phrase that entitled her book, meant that sin resides in bodily pleasure. It is quite possible that Bogan at this age felt on subconscious or even conscious levels some guilt for throwing herself headlong into this disaster of "an unfortunate early marriage" (WWL 6) which she had rushed into to escape her life at home. This is the version of sin according to St. Paul which Bogan read:

I find then a law, that when I have a will to do good, evil is present with me.
For I am delighted with the law of God, according to the inward man:
But I see another law in my members, fighting against the law of my mind, and captivating me in the law of sin, that is in my members.
Unhappy man that I am, who shall deliver me from the body of this death?[21]

The answer for St. Paul is God and faith; presumably at this point in her life Bogan had renounced God in the Catholic sense. Her title is meant to be ironic—pleasure results in terrible pain—but it is impossible to ignore the double ironies of this title for one who was raised a Catholic: Because she has sinned, the pain is deserved. However, Bogan's book is a kind of "bible" for the woman who is trying to work through her feelings after a love affair that has failed. In order to chart the emotional graph, the ups and downs, of this first book and to watch how Bogan expressed herself, we will examine several poems that can be taken as emblematic of the whole. The impulse to chastity is a major theme of *Body of This Death* as it is in Paul. In "Ad Castitatem" (8), Bogan uses simple, stripped, declarative language to invoke chastity as the only answer to love disappointed and denied. Here is the modern poem as prayer; the rhythm is slow, incantatory, as the lover tries to banish flesh. Bogan brings up again what she had learned from writing the earliest poems, the expression of sameness to convey nothingness ("Alike . . . / Lie the fruitful and the barren branch.") The first stanza ends in simplicity, with its pagan offerings (water, stone); the last ends with an echo of both Mallarmé and Yeats. "Hear me, infertile, Beautiful futility" excels in its sonorous repetition of "i's" and "l's." In fact, Elizabeth Frank conjectures that the title of Bogan's first volume owes something to the symbolist tradition as well as to St. Paul. She points to Arthur Symons's essay on Mallarmé in *The Symbolist Movement in Literature:*

> It is the distinction of Mallarmé to have aspired after an impossible liberation of the soul of literature from what is fretting and constraining in "the body of that death," which is the mere literature of words. Words, he has realized, are of value only as a notation of the free breath of the spirit; words, therefore, must be employed with an extreme care, in their choice and adjustment, in setting them to reflect and chime upon one another; yet least of all for their own sake, for what they can never, except by suggestion, express.[22]

Bogan's poems do not aspire to realms as transcendent as Mallarmé's. Her escape is of a different order. It is without long-lined lamentation, the heritage of many of her nineteenth-century female predecessors, that Bogan sings her song of utter devastation. However, her avowal of chastity after failed love links her to these ancestors.

In "Men Loved Wholly Beyond Wisdom" (16), Bogan sounds one of the themes of her controversial "Women" poem—that ". . . when they [women] take life over their door-sills / They should let it go by." (19) Here the only solution to women's unbalanced crazy loving is its unbalanced opposite, complete withdrawal:

> Heart, so subtle now and trembling,
> What a marvel to be wise,
> To love never in this manner!
> To be quiet in the fern

> Like a thing gone dead and still,
> Listening to the prisoned cricket
> Shake its terrible, dissembling
> Music in the granite hill.
>
> (16)

Images of imprisonment are central to *Body of This Death*. The youth, the unconvincing persona of "A Tale," tries to escape his unfulfillment and thus "cuts what holds his days together / And shuts him in, as lock on lock . . ." (BE 3). "The Frightened Man" is entrapped as well:

> In fear of the rich mouth
> I kissed the thin,—
> Even that was a trap
> to snare me in.
>
> (6)

Bogan used the male masks to distance herself from her subject matter, an exercise she perhaps needed in order to go beyond the personal revelation of some of the early uncollected poems. She wants to suggest that the myth of romantic love assails all, and in "Juan's Song," she almost convinces us of the equality of romantic devastation for women and men: "What the wise doubt, the fool believes— / Who is it, then, that love deceives?" (10)

Countering the withdrawal that follows romantic disappointment is the discovery that one is "passionate beyond the will," as in "The Alchemist":

> I burned my life, that I might find
> A passion wholly of the mind,
> Thought divorced from eye and bone,
> Ecstasy come to breath alone.
> I broke my life, to seek relief
> From the flawed light of love and grief.
> With mounting beat the utter fire
> Charred existence and desire.
> It died low, ceased its sudden thresh.
> I had found unmysterious flesh—
> Not the mind's avid substance—still
> Passionate beyond the will.
>
> (15)

With perfect artistic control, Bogan writes of the inability to control. She invokes alchemy by indirection, letting the poem's title stand as a gloss on the doomed attempt to make something pure of the base, here the sensuous life. The poem is perfect in its rhythm and its rhyme, perfect in its juxtaposition of the will to transcend "love and grief" through mind and the assertion of mind's stubborn opposite, sensual need which, after this arduous quest, turns out to be "unmysterious."

Bogan, then, was learning to make the kind of poems she wanted to make, to express feeling in a compact, intense form. Being "strong," while feeling, was a value for her: The kind of balance, strength and sagacity displayed in "The Alchemist" is, however, only momentarily achieved. Rather, self-destructiveness takes over in many poems of *Body of This Death* and in the real experience of many women. In "Portrait," the very young woman feels it is all over for her ("She is possessed by time, who once / Was loved by men" [11]). In "The Crows" "The woman who has grown old / and knows desire must die / Yet turns to love again, / Hears the crows' cry" (16). The woman is archetypal, flinging herself at love against her own better interests, repeating the experience of all the women who have come before her. In "Last Hill in a Vista" the extremism of these either/or attitudes is recognized. The first stanza borders on self-pity, while the second marks, if gently, the decision that leaves "stiff walls" to "choose this more fragile boundary." Here there is an attempt to choose a life of greater sanity and balance, yet the tone of utter sadness at poem's end mirrors loss—the loss, perhaps, of boundless youthful hope.

The wide oscillations of mood, the confusions, of the woman who speaks in *Body of This Death* feel real-to-life: This is the experience of a woman who is forced to come to terms with dead romantic hopes. The poems are poignant precisely because *the woman has no place to stand*. There is no solution. For example, "Chanson un peu naive" is pure cry—and that is no place to stand. Even the defiance that ends the book, although stirring, is conflicted. This first book of poems convinces us that romantic love for women is, quite simply, a trap. *Body of This Death* is emotionally powerful because it captures the woman *in* the experience, before she is able to see around it or outside it. Only momentarily does she come out from under the devastation in, for example, "Sub Contra," a poem about both art and anger ("Let there sound from music's root / One note rage can understand" [5]) and in "My Voice Not Being Proud," which tempts rage but finally undermines it:

> My voice, not being proud
> Like a strong woman's, that cries
> Imperiously aloud
> That death disarm her, lull her—
> Screams for no mourning color
> Laid menacingly, like fire,
> Over my long desire.

It is hard not to mistake this for the nineteenth-century poetess yelling for death after disappointed love but, in fact, this is Bogan's assault on that tradition. Instead of a nineteenth-century death, the speaker chooses something more ironic, more still, more modern:

> As you lie, I shall lie:
> Separate, eased and cured . . .
>   (13)

I hear anger—repressed, defeated—in these lines.

Bogan ends her book with two poems of defiance. In them, she displays her growing artistic control. In title, "Fifteenth Farewell" comments on the number of leave-takings that precede the final one in a romantic situation; in form, it is two sonnets, strikingly different in diction. The first, with its archaic rhetoric, is reminiscent of Shakespeare; the second, spoken simply, harks back to the nature imagery she practiced in her earliest poems. The first sonnet expresses a defiant determination to live, to not go under, to beat the desire for death. It is a little self-dramatizing; and a little surprising for one moment in its final lines (the "blade" and "fang" of love), which bring portents of the sado-masochistic manifestations of love in the next book, *Dark Summer* (1929). In the second sonnet, there is a complete change of tone:

Fifteenth Farewell

II

I erred, when I thought loneliness the wide
Scent of mown grass over forsaken fields,
Or any shadow isolation yields.
Loneliness was the heart within your side.
Your thought, beyond my touch, was tilted air
Ringed with as many borders as the wind.
How could I judge you gentle or unkind
When all bright flying space was in your care?
Now that I leave you, I shall be made lonely
By simple empty days,—never that chill
Resonant heart to strike between my arms
Again, as though distraught for distance,—only
Levels of evening, now, behind a hill,
Or a late cock-crow from the darkening farms.
(24–25)

The warrior of the first sonnet has in the second given in to great sadness. These lines sing of grief and aloneness; the image of tilted air is nothing short of amazing. The poem beautifully expresses the complete vulnerability, the complete trusting—and the turning over of one's soul—which is the mark of romantic love. Coldness and irony come through toward the end ("that chill / Resonant heart"), this all the more striking for its placement in the midst of gentle pain and resignation. The melancholy acceptance of aloneness is archetypal in women's experience, and in women's poetry.

The theme of imprisonment—explicitly registered or lying just beneath the surface of all the poems—emerges with full force in the final selection of the volume, simply titled "Sonnet":

Since you would claim the sources of my thought
Recall the meshes whence it sprang unlimned,
The reedy traps which other hands have timed
To close upon it. Conjure up the hot

Blaze that it cleared so cleanly, or the snow
Devised to strike it down. It will be free.
Whatever nets draw in to prison me
At length your eyes must turn to watch it go.

My mouth, perhaps, may learn one thing too well,
My body hear no echo save its own,
Yet will the desperate mind, maddened and proud,
Seek out the storm, escape the bitter spell
That we obey, strain to the wind, be thrown
Straight to its freedom in the thunderous cloud.

(26)

We associate this diction with the Elizabethan sonnet form: "unlimned," "ready," the charged adjectives of anger ("desperate," "maddened"), bring echoes of previous traditions. This first stanza is viscerally powerful as it uses the animal world to represent the entrapment of a human being. In "The Romantic" the woman had been trapped and her stance was a passive one: "In her obedient breast, all that ran free / You thought to bind, like echoes in a shell" (12). The metaphor leaves the anger enclosed. In this "Sonnet" (printed in italics in the original 1923 version of *Body of This Death*) the trap is sprung. The second stanza of "Sonnet" has body, mouth (the latter a common synecdoche in Bogan, as in "In fear of the rich mouth / I kissed the thin," [6] and "You have put your two hands upon me, and your mouth" [7])—and the mind that would escape. There is more defiance, more anger here than in any other poem in the book. Yet the original trap of the first stanza invades the second. The poem ends ironically in a "freedom" full of danger.

When it surfaced in 1923, *Body of This Death* was not without its admirers. The *New Republic* reviewer wrote:

> It would be so easy to say . . . that Louise Bogan's first book . . . lacks variety of theme because under a multiple dazzle of title and imagery it actually sings one song over and over again. A lyric poem, however, is by its very nature a short cry; and these twenty-seven short cries are each of the very core of gathered intensity. A cry of anguish, however short and however torn from the heart, may be more impressive than the repertory of a barrel organ.[23]

Bogan is lucky that this critic decided not to depend on that staple of criticism of women's work, its lack of range. Just as representative is an assessment such as Mark Van Doren's. He was struck by the technical competence of the work (this is "pure poetry") but he does not know what the poems are about:

> It is impossible to say what she has said. . . . One can be certain that experience of some ultimate sort is behind this writing, that something has been gone through with entirely and intensely, leaving the desolation of a field swept once for all by fire. . . . Miss Bogan has spoken always with intensity and intelligent skill; she has not always spoken clearly. Now and then her poetry comes too immediately from a personal source to mean much to others. . . .[24]

Yet it is surely true that this first book of poems is difficult to interpret. *Body of This Death* has a complicated heritage. It stands between the female tradition and modernist influence. It was written after the poet read the symbolists and Yeats's *Responsibilities* but before she had a literary reputation to protect; her reticence, her obscurity, would increase with the next volume. Bogan strived for the objectivity, the irony she thought of as modern. These marks of modernism, linked with her expressions of female vulnerability, are responsible for the intensity of her first book. It is precisely this combination of compact form and female subject matter that, paradoxically, led some of her contemporaries and many of the present generation away from a work that seems too "obscure."

V.

INTERLUDE
"THE SPRINGS OF POETRY" (1923)

> The poet represses the outright narrative of
> his life. He absorbs it, along with life itself.
> The repressed becomes the poem. Actually,
> I have written down my experience in the
> closest detail. But the rough and vulgar facts
> are not there.
>
> —JAR 72

> . . . the difference between art and the event
> is always absolute . . .
>
> —T. S. Eliot, "Tradition and
> the Individual Talent"

In December 1923, the same month that *Body of This Death* came out, the
twenty-six-year-old Bogan published an essay in the *New Republic* that
showed how completely she had absorbed modernist ideas. By now she was
living in New York City and had found literary friends and editorial work on
the *Measure*. Her life had changed a great deal since the writing of her first
book. She was thinking more consciously and carefully about her standing as
an artist. "The Springs of Poetry" was her first public declaration of what she
thought poetry should be; in writing it, she put herself in the tradition of the
modernist poet-critic. There are, for example, many similarities in the concepts
of poetry advocated in T. S. Eliot's "Tradition and the Individual Talent" and
in Bogan's credo delivered four years later, although no other modernist
declaration rivals hers for drama. Bogan did not hasten to bring attention to
her essay in later years; its hyperbolic cast no doubt caused this suppression.
Yet it took a great deal of self-confidence and self-possession to write the piece;
and she must have worked very hard on it, since "The Springs of Poetry" is a
stunning example of poetic prose. The piece is both declaration and self-
defense. Letters from the period show Bogan's contempt for much of what
passed as poetry in America ("Why get mad about Frost and the Pulitzer? He's
48 or so, and just getting crabbed, so it's better he get it now than later" (To
Rolphe Humphries, 19 May 1924, 7). It illustrated as well a pride in her own

creative efforts ("*The Dial* certainly gave the book [*Body of This Death*] a rotten smack, didn't it? Johnny Weaver in the Brooklyn Eagle put me down as very slight and wanted to know why all the hosannas had been raised . . ." (To Edmund Wilson, 1 Mar. 1924, 5).

Ironically titled, the essay shows how little there was of the bounteous and the liquid and the overflowing in Bogan's experience of creation. It is fascinating for what it reveals of the young poet's attitudes toward her art—the strictness of her ideas of poetry, her severe sense of what was permissible and what was not. Bogan demanded that poetry be personal in the sense of coming out of some real emotional experience. She limited that test of emotional truth further by asserting that not *all* emotions belonged in poetry. Her aesthetic demanded a constant confrontation both with the stuff of the psyche and with the rigors of formalist technique. Not surprising that the poet who sets such high standards for herself will do anything at all to avoid these tests. "The Springs of Poetry" opens this way:

> When he sets out to resolve, as rationally as he may, the tight irrational knot of his emotion, the poet hesitates for a moment. Unless the compulsion be absolute, as is rarely the case, the excitement of the resolution sets in only after this pause, filled with doubt and terror. He would choose anything, rather than the desperate task before him: a book, music, or talk and laughter. Almost immediately the interruption is found, and the emotion diverted, or the poem is begun, and the desperation has its use.[1]

Throughout this little essay, Poetry is male. Its language is as terrifying as the Ancients' evocation of the power and dread of poetic inspiration and as rigorously demanding as Eliot's idea of the poetic process which fuses thought and emotion. Bogan goes on to invoke Aristotle directly: "The author of the *Poetica* recognized this necessary intensity when he wrote that distress and anger are most faithfully portrayed by one who is feeling them at the moment, that poetry demands a man with a special gift for it, or else one with a touch of madness in him." This idea of an absolute compulsion to write, of all that one did not allow oneself to write or to let others see, remained with Bogan throughout her poetic life. She was a most severe critic of her own work; this was one aspect of her aesthetic of limitation. The poet lets many potential poems slip by because (s)he does not truly feel this primal necessity and "even a poet has a great many uses for grief and anger beyond putting them into a poem. . . ." The poem emerges from a real emotional situation but is not reality itself. ("The poem is always a last resort. In it the poet makes a world in little, and finds peace, even though, under complete focused emotion, the evocation be far more bitter than reality, or far more lovely.") Eliot makes similar demands: "[Poetry] is a concentration, and a new thing resulting from the concentration. . . ."[2] Further, poetry "is an expression of significant emotion, emotion which has its life in the poem and not in the history of the poet" (11). Or so Eliot would have us believe.

Because it is exhausting and impossible to stay constantly at the high pitch of energy and intensity modernist poetry demands, the poet avoids the confrontation. He is almost world-weary from the demands, for "his hand has become chilled, from being held too long against the ground to feel how it is cold; his mind flinches at cutting down once again into the dark with the knife of irony or analysis." Again: a woman poet writes using the male pronoun; in fact, the modernist male tradition stands behind such declarations. We hear the early Mallarmé of high-flown diction and disgust with life ("Las du triste hôpital . . .")[3] and the Eliot of intellect and distance. The knife, like the pen, is a male instrument; the wo-man poet inevitably uses the knife/pen against herself. After her second breakdown, Bogan called it "the knife of the perfectionist attitude in art and life at my throat . . ." (27 July 1934, 79).

Before Eliot and Bogan, the French symbolists had decreed that the poem comes out of experience but is never the experience itself. "Peindre non la chose mais l'effect qu'elle produit," wrote Mallarmé ("Paint not the thing itself but the effect it produces").[4] This is Bogan's delineation of the same idea:

> Even though at its best a poem cannot come straight out of the heart, but must break away in some oblique fashion from the body of sorrow or joy,—be the mask not the incredible face,—yet the synthetic poem can never be more than a veil dropped before a void. It may sound, to change the images, in ears uninitiate to the festival, but never to those, who, having once heard, can recognize again the maenad cry.

Echoes once again of modernist poetry and its forerunners: the masks of Yeats, the veils and voids of the French symbolists. But enter, suddenly, in this world of 'the poet he,' a female figure and it is the figure of madness: the maenad, the Dionysiac frenzied, raging woman. At the beginning of the essay, Bogan reminds us that Aristotle knew the poet had a bit of madness in him. The artifact, the poem, is nothing compared to the *real* sound of the maenad cry, that profound source of poetry which few, perhaps only the poets, hear. Violence, then, and a kind of destruction, are necessary to creation. "Women cannot create because they are unwilling to destroy," Anaïs Nin once wrote. Poetry, moreover, is a kind of punishment, as the aesthetic and ascetic merge; in order to prevent him/herself from letting out inferior work, the poet must subject him/herself to the most severe surroundings:

> One would wish for the poet a stern countryside that could claim him completely, identify him rigidly as its own under the color of every season. He should be blessed by the power to write behind clenched teeth, to subsidize his emotion by every trick and pretense so that it trickle out through other channels, if it be not essential to speech,—blessed too, by a spirit as loud as a houseful of alien voices, ever tortured and divided with itself.

The poet is blessed with a gift; this belief in "génie" places Bogan squarely in the romantic tradition. The verb is used ironically as well, since the celebrated tortures and divisions of modern life reside within the "blessed" poet and it is out of this tension that s/he makes the modernist poem. The spring trickles as the poet *prevents* all but the most precious from entering the poem. It is reticence, the holding back that makes the modern poem:

> Under the power of such reticence, in which passion is made to achieve its own form, definite and singular, those poems were written that keep an obscure name still alive, or live when the name of their author is forgotten. Speaking thus, as though the very mind has a tongue, Yeats achieves his later work: poems terribly beautiful, in which the hazy adverbial quality has no place, built of sentences reduced to the bones of noun, verb, and preposition.

This shall be the standard for her next book, *Dark Summer* (1929):

> This is the further, the test simplicity, in the phrase of Alice Meynell, sprung from the passion of which every poet will always be afraid, but to which he should vow himself forever.

The fear is explicit in this final passage. Through the modernist poem, a kind of immortality is achieved that subverts death. For Bogan, as for so many modernist poets, the subject was a life lived without the prospect of an afterlife in the old sense of the word; but the trick they played on death was art. Male poets knew they had a chance to live on in this way; few women poets had this chance. How many have heard of Alice Meynell, or Louise Bogan for that matter? The *Dark Summer* poems Bogan was beginning as she wrote this essay were for her a confrontation with some of the great themes of modernist male poetry—the death imbedded in life, as seen by those who had determined "to live *without the need for philosophy*" (JAR 58).

Modernism served Bogan in many ways. It helped her to tame her emotional excesses by giving her forms for contained emotion. It answered her own perfectionism and severity: Passion and control could live together. And by vowing herself to it forever, she hoped to accomplish what few women poets before her had achieved—a place among the poets whose names, once obscure, live on.

VI.

"A LABOR OF TEARS"

DARK SUMMER (1929)

> There are so many ways one can't let
> oneself feel, in poetry. But that's all to the
> good. Maidie wants me to write some
> happy poems.
>
> (To Rolphe Humphries, 21 June 1938, 172)

Of all Bogan's books, *Dark Summer* is surely the hardest to comprehend. In one of the more sensitive reviews of Bogan's collected work, Elder Olsen, in 1954, wrote:

> . . . the personages of these poems appear to us as they might by a lightning flash, or as they might be glimpsed from a swift train; they are caught in attitudes obviously significant, which we cannot interpret, they make gestures passionate but mysterious . . . her poems are like pictures or scenes from some passionate and bitter play which we have not seen; the decor is brilliantly clear, the characters are fixed in poses which betray much, if only we could interpret.[1]

This characterization applies more to *Dark Summer* than to any other volume. Most obviously, it is a book about the inevitable passage of time, using summer, usually associated with life and fullness, as metaphor for the cruel inevitability of death. Like *Body of This Death*, this book is shot through with negation; but now it is the ironic voice of the older woman of experience that we hear. The title poem evokes a sense of impending chaos and destruction:

Dark Summer

Under the thunder-dark, the cicadas resound.
The storm in the sky mounts, but is not yet heard.
The shaft and the flash wait, but are not yet found.
The apples that hang and swell for the late comer,
The simple spell, the rite not for our word,
The kisses not for our mouths,—light the dark summer.

(49)

The sense of negation, the arrested, and ultimately unfulfilled expectation, dominate this volume. With simple language and slow, measured lines, with light and sound, Bogan expresses one of the classic themes of poetry. An understanding of death comes through the experience of love: Love, like life, does not last. It passes and changes and is not what we would expect when young; with each attempt at love, we grow older, in body and mind. These are the dark themes of *Dark Summer*. These classical themes are deepened by Bogan's particular experience of love, an experience that made the book incomprehensible to many of the critics who read *Dark Summer* when it first appeared in 1929. The woman who stands behind the *Dark Summer* poems is certain that she will be betrayed in love. For Bogan, this obsession originated in her own mother's fulsome affection and then her sudden disappearance. The fear of betrayal leads to a kind of sado-masochistic attitude to relation; the best defense against betrayal is to betray first. Particularly in her second marriage, Bogan alternated between being tyrant and submissive partner:

> . . . what has never been explained thoroughly by me to you is the really dreadful emotional state I was trapped in for many years—a state which Raymond struggled manfully against, I will say, for a long time. In those days, my devotion came out all counter-clockwise, as it were. I was a *demon* of jealousy, for example; and a sort of *demon* of fidelity, too: "morbid fidelity," Dr. Wall came to call it. A slave-maker, really, while remaining a sort of slave. Dreadful! Thank God v. little of it got into the poems; but the general warp showed up in every detail of my life. Except for a certain saving *humor*, I should have indeed been a full *monster*. (To May Sarton, 28 Jan. 1954, 282)

At its most extreme, this obsession provoked the desire to hurt and to be hurt. Out of this pain came a kind of pleasure:

> When it is over, you say to yourself: 'Never possibly can I feel that way again.' It is like a wild beast in the heart, that turns its prey over slowly, seeing the soft places, the tender places between bone and bone, the yielding muscle and soft flesh, wherein the teeth may sink. It is at once the victim and the beast. Quietly they lie together, on fresh grass, and again enter the slow struggle, the torture beyond feeling. The dead yet living victim is turned; the eater seeks slowly, passionately, the next place in which to set its fang. The wounds are made but do not bleed.
> Just afterward, a mood of pity descends on the freshly punished spirit. . . . (JAR 130)

This passage from the "Journals of a Poet" was written in 1959 and published posthumously in the *New Yorker* in 1978. In it, Bogan captures an experience of domination and submission in which partners alternate for sexual power. In fact, as Bogan was learning as she wrote *Dark Summer,* the artist-woman has an extremely problematic relationship to sexual love. The standard model for heterosexual love demands a dominant male and a submissive female. The powerful woman artist cannot survive this inequality in love; yet the patterns and expectations for love are so deeply ingrained in both women and men that relationships get worked out in all kinds of queer ways as partners attempt to conform to deeply embedded patterns. The agonies of passion for gifted women are chillingly detailed in the work of women writers. For example, one can find experience like Bogan's in Jean Rhys's *Wide Sargasso Sea* and in Gayle Jones's *Eva's Man.* And in H.D.'s compelling and painful roman à clef, *Bid Me to Live,* the artist Julia (H.D.) is devastated because her husband leaves her, the cold woman artist, for a warm, real (younger) woman. In the novel Julia recognizes the impossibility of accepting love defined in male terms. In the following passage of *Bid Me to Live,* Frederico is the foil for D. H. Lawrence, with whom H.D. had an intense relationship but probably not an affair:

> There was one loophole, one might be an artist. Then the danger met the danger, the woman was man-woman, the man was woman-man. But Frederico, for all his acceptance of her verses, had shouted his man-is-man, his woman-is-woman at her; his shrill peacock-cry sounded a love cry, death-cry for their generation.[2]

To write about this experience was a way out of the living death of this kind of male-defined sexual relation. It took enormous strength and insight for H.D. to come to terms with the consequences for her of the ideas of one of the love prophets of the modern age, ideas that are an extension of the cult of the phallic which has dominated Western thought for centuries. For, according to male ideas, women must give away their power in order to experience love. To compare male fantasies of heterosexual love with female experiences as they are conveyed in literature by women is a sobering pursuit indeed. Nor is it easy to look at the forms neurosis takes in women poets. Perhaps at some point in literary history we will be able to put the female experiences of intimacy, including insights both into heterosexual and lesbian relation, beside the enormous knowledge we have of the personal lives of our male writers, from the fetishes of the probably impotent Baudelaire to the idealizations of Mallarmé to the barren passions of Yeats and the exploitations of wives and daughters in Robert Lowell. This would bring us, surely, a full and often sordid picture of heterosexual relation but one we might use to think and feel more realistically and honestly about sexuality.

Bogan's "The Flume" is explicit about the obsession with betrayal that poisoned her love life. "The Flume" appeared in the 1929 edition of *Dark Summer* but was not reprinted in succeeding collections and, in fact, Bogan predicted, "When I'm dead, someone will gather it up and insert it in the works, I suppose, with notes!" (To Ruth Limmer, 23 Nov. 1956, 8, n1). Fortunately, Ruth Limmer has included "The Flume" and the poet's notes about it in *Journey Around My Room* (59–67). This commentary will provide the notes Bogan dreaded, for as is surely clear by now, I do not agree with Bogan's severe editing of her oeuvre, because I find much that is valuable for an understanding of her work and of women's poetry in her suppressed poems.

"The Flume" differs from most of the poems of *Dark Summer* both in its form and its direct delineation of the agonies of female passion. This long narrative poem tells the story of a woman with a shadowy past who is now married to a "good" man but who remains restless still. She keeps looking for reasons to doubt the man's sincerity. "The Flume" opens with these lines:

> She had a madness in her for betrayal.
> She looked for it in every room in the house.
> Sometimes she thought she must rip the floor to find
> A box, a letter, a ring, to set her grief,
> So long a rusty wheel, revolving in her fury.
>
> (JAR 60)

Childhood memories inspired "The Flume." Among Bogan's notes as she worked on the poem is this: "The Flume cascaded down the rocks, with bright sun sparkling on the clear, foamy water. My mother was afraid of the flume. It had voices for her; it called her and beckoned her. So I, too, began to fear it" (JAR 59–60). Bogan's mother pursued passion in an age when women were not supposed to admit to sexual feeling. Women have often pursued passion in order to express their defiance of social mores; in fact, rebellion through sexuality has been one of women's most common strategies. For many women, great guilt is the inevitable aftermath of this strategy. In "The Flume" the woman seeks betrayal because then she will be punished, as she should, for overweening passion. ("She had some guilt in her to be betrayed, / She had the terrible hope he could not love her" [62].) In part II of the poem the sound of thunder is a metaphor for the woman's love and fear of the dangers of passion, and in part III we begin to understand that for this woman, forbidden passion has no warmth in it.

> Again she remembers
> The true hard cold that caught at the wild girl's body,
> When night after night she felt the autumn break
> And open the country she knew, when she gave her kisses
> Beside rough field-stones piled into a wall
> Cold as the wind in every particle.
>
> (64–65)

This wild, rebellious woman wants freedom and goes after it in the only way she knows how. The search in this form is doomed.

"The Flume" is remarkable both for its evocation of passion and place. Bogan did not like it partly because it ends so quickly, with the obsession gone. She wrote years later:

> I have never been quite sure about "The Flume." It came from the right place, and I worked hard on it, and it has some nice moments—the hot stove and the no-sound of water which were actually observed and lived with, at one period of my life. Perhaps I have the feeling that one doesn't get out of that kind of obsession so easily—the "facts" are false, at the end. . . . (To Ruth Limmer, 23 Nov. 1956, 8, n1)

In the last section of "The Flume," the young woman is able to feel the power of generous love and to succumb to it. The furious fear of betrayal has been replaced by passivity and the flume is quiet:

> Soon he will find her,
> Still dressed for flight, quiet upon his bed . . .
> She will lie here
> Hearing at last the timbre of love and silence.
> (67)

In "The Flume" the experiences of mother and daughter mesh. The demon of jealousy/demon of fidelity syndrome in which Bogan found herself caught is registered in several short, tense poems that remained in her collections. It would be hard to understand the emotions that stand behind a poem like "Tears in Sleep" without knowledge of "The Flume" and of Bogan's particular demons. Here the speaker is perversely determined to undermine chances for happiness in love:

Tears in Sleep

> All night the cocks crew, under a moon like day,
> And I, in the cage of sleep, on a stranger's breast,
> Shed tears, like a task not to be put away—
> In the false light, false grief in my happy bed,
> A labor of tears, set against joy's undoing.
> I would not wake at your word, I had tears to say.
> I clung to the bars of the dream and they were said,
> And pain's derisive hand had given me rest
> From the night giving off flames, and the dark renewing.
> (44)

The imagery suggests that we are imprisoned by our obsessions, which make strangers of friends; the speaker is absolutely determined to be unhappy. A concordance to Bogan's poetry would produce "grief," that old word, one with rich and deep literary association, as one of the recurring motifs of this volume. The grief-producing obsession lies deep within the unconscious, in the depths of dream, and the masochism is complete: For the speaker, pain is life-giving. The mental anguish of neurotic compulsion is violently brought forth in "Fiend's Weather." ("O embittered joy, / You fiend in fair weather, / Foul winds from secret quarters / Howl here together" [49].) The secrets begin in childhood and as adults we guard them most privately; they emerge in the expression of sexuality. In "Fiend's Weather" there is the sense of something uncontrollable that keeps coming back, childhood furies revisiting in adult life. As adults, we try to understand those experiences of childhood we find ourselves repeating as we grow older, and we fight to grow out of them. This is what "If We Take All Gold" grapples with; "That which we thought precious" and discover undermines us, we seek to put away, to "store sorrow's gold" (30). One must first dredge up that gold in order to look at it and to understand it and *then* store it away, forever. It is this kind of understanding that is Bogan's gift, in *Dark Summer:* the necessity to confront, then banish, the demons of our past. We can go on repeating those neurotic patterns learned in childhood and if we do, we remain children; maturity means relinquishing those learned habits, releasing our grip on "the bars of the dream" ("Tears in Sleep," 44). The trick is to come out of the process, not embittered, but capable of love.

Part of what Bogan, like many women, had to confront, were those states of either wild passion, as in "The Drum" or in "Feuernacht," where passion "has burned all" (36), or their opposite, the attitudes of self-pitying resignation, as in "Girl's Song" and "Second Song" with its echoes of *Body of This Death:*

> I said out of sleeping:
> Passion, farewell.
> Take from my keeping,
> Bauble and shell,
>
> Black salt, black provender,
> Tender your store
> To a new pensioner,
> To me no more.
>
> (37)

This mood of resignation does not dominate the volume, however. *Dark Summer* is a book of the eyes that would turn away but, above all, a book that tries to see experience clearly. In the chilling symbolist image of the cold "Winter Swan" that introduces the volume, summer ends with "the eyes in hiding" (29). In "Division," "The burden of the seen / Is clasped against the eye" (32), bringing the sense of self watching self and trapped immobile in the watching. In "Feuernacht," with the burning gone wild, "the shuttered eye" blinded by wild passion is at last opened to look at the fire: "The eye in its lair / Quivers for sight," with the preposition meaning both "in order to" and "because" (36). "She gives most dangerous sight / To keep his life awake" in "For a Marriage" (43). In "Simple Autumnal" "the tearless eyes" will not confront grief (40); in "Didactic Piece" endings—of seasons, of life—are faced:

> Let the allegiance go; the tree and the hard bud seed themselves.
> The end is set, whether it be sought or relinquished.
> We wait, we hear, facing the mask without eyes,
> Grief without grief, facing the eyeless music.
>
> (42)

The complexity of language registers the complexity of idea—all that we will not look at, that which we do open our eyes to—and that which we would face, but can never see.

There is a kind of conscious artistry at work in *Dark Summer* that we did not see in *Body of This Death;* the imagery of the seasons, of death and renewal, inspired by her life in the country, is consistent throughout the volume. The book shows Bogan trying out new ways of speaking; she finally abandoned the long-lined poems but kept the examples of the "narrow lyric," such as "Late"; she experimented with a new voice in the Baroque-like opulence of language of "Didactic Piece" and "Simple Autumnal." In the latter poem, autumn is emblematic of an unwillingness to let grief have its season; the grief is not named, nor need it be, since the insight is that we must take time to grieve loss and pain in all its forms and if we do not life cannot move on. This sagacity is given depth through weighty, slow-moving lines and the imagery of an arrested fall season. In *Dark Summer* Bogan explores classical themes of mutability. The change of seasons, the passage of time, and death are inevitable. The volume is deepened and personalized by Bogan's confrontations with her own demons, as in "Late" and "Division." Poetry has typically linked ideas of death with those of love, for it is often through the experience of love that one understands that nothing lasts. This is Bogan's dominant view of romantic love throughout her poetry. "For a Marriage" almost inverts the sentiment we would expect in a poem of that title. Its dominant imagery, a sword, suggests both masculinity and destruction. The sense of reciprocity—that she keeps him awake and alive and that in exchange he protects her from her own demons—is finally a reciprocity that is self-enclosing, two in heterosexual relation hiding out from the world. Loneliness, neurosis, are hidden from view: This is Bogan's poem "For a Marriage."

The poet of *Dark Summer* is a quite different woman from the one who wrote *Body of This Death*. When young, we think that time will stretch out without term; in middle age, we wonder where time has gone and are faced with all those parts of our life we were going to change. We now realize that change will not just happen. Jaqueline Ridgeway tells us that in an unpublished short story, "Half a Letter," Bogan describes youth as the time of living in the future, seen in dramatic, important terms. But when older, "We are literally ourselves, and things function literally around us, terribly apparent and undisguised."[3] *Dark Summer* grapples with time's truths, the paradox of time that passes and time that stands still, if we do not act upon it. "Late" is a rendering of this knowledge:

Late

The cormorant still screams
Over cave and promontory.
Stony wings and bleak glory
Battle in your dreams.
Now sullen and deranged,
Not simply, as a child,
You look upon the earth
And find it harrowed and wild.
Now, only to mock
At the sterile cliff laid bare,
At the cold pure sky unchanged,
You look upon the rock,
You look upon the air.

(39)

One might mistake this for an early imagist poem by H.D., both for its emotional tenor and its "narrow lyric" form. Yet Yeats is the model; this, in the language of "The Springs of Poetry," is that idea of a poem without adverbs, "reduced to the bones of noun, verb, and preposition." "Late" is remarkable for its sound. The bird is predatory and frightening, all the more so for the suggestion of double-entendre we hear in the French: "corps mourant" (dying body). The repeated "o" sounds produce a decidedly eerie effect. "Late" is frightening through its imagery and because of its truth: Childhood demons brought into adult life change their aspect—and sooner or later we must confront them or stay hollow. In *Dark Summer* an end point is reached; the despair is so great that one wonders where the poet can go.

At the end of a volume that has inverted metaphor and seen summer's richness as a kind of ruse that momentarily makes us forget mutability and death, Bogan places a long narrative poem, "Summer Wish," which tries to give hope a voice. The final poem of *Dark Summer* is a dialogue of the "gentle self split up," a struggle between death and life or, as Bogan put it at a reading in later life, between nature and human experience.[4] It is also a modern woman's confrontation with truths brought up from the unconscious. Bogan wrote the poem when the rest of *Dark Summer* was about to go to press. Its drama lies in the conflict between the self that wants to believe in "summer," a kind of pledge of faith for the future, and another self whose experience says there is little to hope for. The two voices try to reason with each other; the first is the voice of negation, which asserts, full of irony, that experience only brings death closer:

> A wish like a hundred others.
> You cannot, as once, yearn forward. The blood now never
> Stirs hot to memory, or to the fantasy
> Of love, with which, both early and late, one lies
> As with a lover.
>
> (54)

The second voice tries to look at the world with optimism, as it catalogues nature's bounty. This hope is constantly undercut by the voice that says no because it is trapped in the past. Time is the major theme of "Summer Wish." What do we do with the past? We cannot entirely forget it but we also must move beyond it. An obsession with the past makes the present unbearable; as we have seen, it is this obsession that is behind the anguish of the love poems of *Dark Summer*. The future stretches before us; but we can have little hope for it if we are stuck in the images of childhood. The violence of that past is brought into adult life:

> First Voice
>
> Memory long since put by,—to what end the dream
> That drags back lived-out life with the wrong words,
> The substitute meaning?
> Those that you once knew there play out false time,

Elaborate yesterday's words, that they were deaf to,
Being dead ten years.—Call back in anguish
The anger in childhood that defiled the house
In walls and timber with its violence?
Now must you listen again
To your own tears, shed as a child, hold the bruise
With your hand, and weep, fallen against the wall,
And beg, *Don't, don't,* while the pitiful rage goes on
That cannot stem itself?
Or, having come into woman's full estate,
Enter the rich field, walk between the bitter
Bowed grain, being compelled to serve
To heed unchecked in the heart the reckless fury
That tears fresh day from day, destroys its traces,—
Now bear the blow too young?

(55)

These seemingly uncontrollable compulsions dating from the violence experienced in childhood end in a wildly destructive attitude toward adult love. (There is even a suggestion of what we now call "child abuse.") Bogan is unrelenting in her dissection of the love/hate (and more hate than love) of this particular kind of animal passion:

First Voice

Not memory, and not the renewed conjecture
Of passion that opens the breast, the unguarded look
Flaying clean the raped defense of the body,
Breast, bowels, throat, now pulled to the use of the eyes
That see and are taken. The body that works and sleeps,
Made vulnerable, night and day, to delight that changes
Upon the lips that taste it, to the lash of jealousy
Stuck on the face, so the betraying bed
Is gashed clear, cold on the mind, together with
Every embrace that agony dreads but sees
Open as the love of dogs.

(56)

As it would have been difficult for the young woman of "The Flume" to get out of her obsession, one wonders how the first voice can ever find its way out of this particular pit. Does guilt engender a revulsion of the flesh? Even as "The Flume" is unconvincing, so too, I find the close of "Summer Wish," as lovely as it is, sudden and more wish-fulfillment than real.

Bogan's letters are never quite as dark as her poems; and in reading them, we discover that what saved her was a sense of humor and a capacity to love, which got buried sometimes but which, miraculously, kept springing up again and again. It is something like this—the capacity for laughter, the capacity to love—and, above all, an incredible *courage,* that Bogan expresses, as the first voice takes on a new timbre at the close of the poem:

Speak out the wish like music, that has within it
The horn, the string, the drum pitched deep as grief.
Speak it like laughter, outward. O brave, O generous
Laughter that pours from the well of the body and draws
The bane that cheats the heart: aconite, nightshade,
Hellebore, hyssop, rue,—symbols and poisons
We drink, in fervor, thinking to gain thereby
Some difference, some distinction. . . .
. . . Though it be for sleep at night,
Speak out the wish.

(58–59)

This is an attempt to come to terms with the tragic dimensions of existence, an acceptance of life and the death within it. The poem ends, in movement and strength and ambiguity:

Second Voice

See now
Open above the field, stilled in wing-stiffened flight,
The stretched hawk fly.

(59)

Bogan felt she had ended her book on a slightly hopeful note. There is flight, surely, but it is the flight of a bird of prey. The general impression of *Dark Summer* stays with us: This is an experience of absence and negation and despair, a book of great intensity and depth which, like much great poetry, reveals itself only with attentive and repeated readings. Its complexity did not get through to most reviewers of the period. This is L. W. Dodd in the *Yale Review* in 1930:

> We have fallen in verse upon finicky and constricted times. Dour and cryptic little poets are making notes for each other on the immediate status of their personal disillusions and disgusts. They do not address the profane vulgar and would hate themselves even more tenderly if we could understand them. They have a secret sign language of their own; they are tense, crabbed and cerebral. However, Miss Louise Bogan is certainly not the least among them, for she can write with a condensed exquisite haughtiness of her immense distaste for life. . . .[5]

That Bogan was capable of a disgust for life is undeniable, although she fought that tendency in herself; "Summer Wish" is one record of that struggle. I do agree there is "a secret sign language" in *Dark Summer*. It is impossible to know how many poets Dodd includes in his dismissal since a "distaste for life" and obscurity are surely two of the marks of modernism. It is clear, however, that there has been less willingness on the part of critics to decipher the meanings of women poets.

Dark Summer is the result both of Bogan's own anguish and of her idea of what she wanted her second book to be, an example of that reticence and severity, that intensity and simplicity she had advocated in "The Springs of Poetry." These conflicts, this perfectionism, would ultimately prove to be too exhausting even for one of her strength.

VII.

"ALONE AND STRONG IN MY PEACE"
THE SLEEPING FURY (1937)

Paula is very much infected by modern
notions. . . . In art, Paula is certainly gifted,
I am astonished by her progress. But if only
this were joined with more humane virtues.
It must be the most difficult thing for a
woman to be highly developed spiritually
and to be intelligent, and still be completely
feminine.

—Otto Modersohn-Becker

But you, fierce delicate tender touch,
Betrayed and hurt me overmuch,

For whom I lagged with what a crew
O far too long, and poisoned through!

—"Spirit's Song," 86

Those hours when murderous wounds are
    made,
Often in joy.

—"Psychiatrist's Song," 134

If *Body of This Death* (1923) is Louise Bogan's most immediate volume and
Dark Summer (1929) at once metaphysical and deeply subjective, then *The
Sleeping Fury* is her most consciously "psychological" work. Through it, she
confronts the demons she had begun to understand by writing *Dark Summer*.

The Sleeping Fury issued out of a period of great crisis for Bogan. Packed
into this slim volume is a woman's experience of a failed second marriage, two
breakdowns, and a coming to terms with her mother. It is thus an extraordinarily painful volume to confront. For a woman, to read some male
writers is to experience great aesthetic pleasure but also to feel a certain

distance because the events, the point of view, are not personally familiar. No
such escape is possible with *The Sleeping Fury.*

In order to understand *The Sleeping Fury,* we need to look in some detail at
both the external and internal events of Bogan's life in the period between
1930 and 1937. The Holden house in northern New York burned to the
ground in 1930 and Bogan lost all her manuscripts. Although she did not
throw up loud public lamentation ("We are really quite well. Do not think us
tragic figures" [6 Jan. 1930, 55]), for a writer the loss of works-in-progress and
books and letters is incalculable. She and Holden then moved from the
tranquilities of the countryside back to New York City. Bogan released only
three poems in 1930 and 1931. "Song" (63), first published in 1930, harks
back to the imagery and tone of passive resignation of *Body of This Death* and
is at the same time a portent of the collapse of marriage, a second time around.
"Song" would become the first poem of *The Sleeping Fury:*

Song

It is not now I learn
To turn the heart away
From the rain of a wet May
Good for the grass and leaves.
Years back I paid my tithe
And earned my salt in kind,
And watched the long slow scythe
Move where the grain is lined,
And saw the stubble burn
Under the darker sheaves.
Whatever now must go
It is not the heart that grieves.
It is not the heart—the stock,
The stone,—the deaf, the blind—
That sees the birds in flock
Steer narrowed to the wind.

(63)

Here is Louise Bogan again mistress of the narrow lyric and the sad song. It
is as though Bogan's memory of disappointment—that first severe disappointment registered in *Body of This Death*—calls up the language of that book.
There are echoes of the experienced woman of "The Crows," who still wants
love although she should know better ("She is a stem long hardened, / A weed
that no scythe mows"). There is the imagery of charred ruins of that poem
("bitter / Winter-burning in the fields" [17]) and of several others in her first
volume ("Ad Castitatem," "Men Loved Wholly Beyond Wisdom") in which
flames and burning are the central metaphor for the ruins of passion. In *Dark
Summer* the fire had gotten out of control: "Sworn to lick at a little / It has
burned all" ("Feuernacht," [36]). Sandra Cookson notes that this "image
belongs to Bogan's youth, and it disappears from her poems after the beautiful
lyric of 1930, entitled "Song," in which the speaker attempts to renounce an
impulse to sexual passion. . . ."[1] In "Summer Wish" the poet had tried to
believe in flight; here, she is again fully in the female mode, resigned to the

limited life. The tone of "Song," wistful, sad, but without cleansing anger, is typical of Bogan's oeuvre as it is of the nineteenth-century woman poet. Moreover, this is the famous "psychology of women" described and prescribed in its Freudian version. Women's choice is "between finding bliss in suffering or peace in renunciation," wrote Helene Deutsch.[2]

In 1931 Bogan had her first "breakdown," a breakdown that was "about" both art and love: She could not write except out of deep personal experience, and reflection upon her life brought up unbearable truths. In April 1931 she entered the Neurological Institute in New York City. She wrote to her publisher, able, miraculously, to be at once funny and analytical about her situation:

> I missed the Psychiatric Institute, or whatever it is, by a hair . . . I refused to fall apart, so I have been taken apart, like a watch. I can truthfully say that the fires of hell can hold no terrors for me now. (11 Apr. 1931, 57)

Here is a proud woman doing what women do, holding herself together through commanding will, refusing to let herself be defeated. Bogan spent a month in a sanitarium in Connecticut, where she wrote "Hypocrite Swift." One of her finest bitter lyrics, published in 1931, also issues from this period:

Henceforth, From the Mind

Henceforth, from the mind,
For your whole joy, must spring
Such joy as you may find
In any earthly thing,
And every time and place
Will take your thought for grace.

Henceforth, from the tongue,
From shallow speech alone,
Comes joy you thought, when young,
Would wring you to the bone,
Would pierce you to the heart
And spoil its stop and start.

Henceforward, from the shell,
Wherein you heard, and wondered
At oceans like a bell
So far from ocean sundered—
A smothered sound that sleeps
Long lost within lost deeps,

Will chime you change and hours,
The shadow of increase
Will sound you flowers
Born under troubled peace—
Henceforth, henceforth
Will echo sea and earth.

(64)

Much of the power of the poem lies in its hollow sounds. In a disciplined iambic tetrameter line, the poet looks hard at the difference between youthful ideas of joy and adult reality. Joy must now be searched out in new places but, in a bitter ironic twist, this does not feel like "joy" at all because it is different from what was dreamed of and expected. For William Jay Smith, there is some repose in poetry to be found here; though it be only "shallow speech" (that is, not life itself) this, he thinks, "is a poem about poetry, about the poet who puts all of life, all her experience of the earth into poetry, and in the end becomes the earth itself."[3] This would surely place the poem in the romantic tradition. It may also be seen in terms of the female tradition because of its resignation. (Perhaps as adults we call this "acceptance.") In the amazing third stanza of the poem, the shell, which for the young woman was an emblem of simple, natural wonders, has been transformed into an image of the necessity to listen to the deep underlying causes of difficulty. In *Body of This Death*, we believed the resignation momentary, issuing as it did from the romantic voice of a young woman; here, it is more profound—and more tragic—because this is the voice of experience. In the early poems, the choice seemed to present itself as passionate love or nothing. In "Henceforth, From the Mind" the woman is older and aware of complexity. Conflict lies deeply repressed; an approach to "reality" involves an acceptance of conflict, that is, the "troubled peace." The poem builds to a crescendo of defeat (and the change in the opening iamb from "henceforth" to "henceforward" extends the agony). We are left with a terrible sense of emptiness, as the woman poet asserts the split between mind and body and renounces passion yet again.

The insights derived through poetry and breakdown were not yet enough for Bogan to leave Holden. She went back to him after her sanitarium cure; at that point, she blamed the problems in her marriage on herself and felt proud that she could still love (even as there was still some measure of shame and guilt in acts of love):

> What ever happens after this, I shall no longer sneer and fleer. One of my component parts, strangely enough, turned out to be the capacity to love. I still can love. Isn't that wonderful? I still can go into love humbly and take it, no matter to what end, and feel humble and ashamed [?]: 'Love comes in at the eyes'—A pretty pass for one of my stiff-necked pride, don't you think? It comes in at the eyes and subdues the body. An army with banners. My God, every poet in the world knew about it, except me. (11 April 1931, 57)

Here is Bogan being sanguine, believing what she fervently wants to believe. Karen Horney would call this "the overvaluation of love." In 1934 Horney wrote that

> women who nowadays obey the impulse to the independent development of their abilities are able to do so only at the cost of a struggle against both external opposition and such resistances within themselves as are created by an intensification of the exclusively sexual function of women.[4]

If a woman is creative and ambitious, it is all the more imperative that she be successful in heterosexual relation—or she loses her claims to "womanhood." Horney observed that the creative women who were her patients in the thirties seemed to oscillate from "the extreme of complete repudiation of femininity on the one hand to the opposite extreme of total rejection of intellectual or vocational activities on the other."[5] These kinds of dilemmas are archetypal for the woman artist and each sought a "solution": Emily Dickinson, for example, chose seclusion and Elizabeth Barrett Browning feigned invalidism. Paula Modersohn-Becker tried to respond to artistic revolution and bourgeois expectation. (She died after giving birth to a daughter.) As a "modern" woman, Bogan no doubt felt that she should not have to make such choices or sacrifices. Yet she, too, oscillated between a devotion to love and work. Nor did she see her dilemmas in the context of a larger problem, the problem of the woman artist. She would no doubt have been helped by such perceptions, as H.D. was. In April she had been proud of her capacity to love and in June she swore by her work. After her first breakdown, she wrote to Harriet Monroe. She knew that she was not well:

> I am much better, although by no means completely well. Several mechanisms have broken down and a strange new period has set in, in my heart and mind. I feel at once renewed and disinherited. Different people say different things. My doctor insists that I love; Robert Frost, whom we saw recently, recommends fear and hatred. But I have lost faith in universal panaceas—work is the one thing in which I really believe. (23 June 1931, 59)

"Renewed, disinherited": a pointed phrase for the results of exhausting psychic confrontations. By January 1932 things were out of control again. This mad epistle went to her good friend Morton Zabel, when she couldn't get out an article:

> I fight in all sorts of ways. I fight by tearing into pieces my whole pride and character, and by smashing everything slick in sight. You cannot think what life with a shell resolves into. All this leaves very little margin for creative effort. (And that sentence is the mope and mow of the jolly grinner in the soul who can keep even misery and malevolence sane.)
>
> Not a *femme fatale*, Morton. Only people with a good wide streak of *chi-chi* and attitudinizing can manage that. Believe, believe that I am proof against my own obsessions. There's mature irony in these bones, my good sir. When the time comes—in the twenty supposititious poems, perhaps—it will serve. *For certain moments at the least, that crafty demon and that loud beast that plague me day and night Ran out of my sight; . . . I saw my freedom won and all laugh in the sun.* (23 Jan. 1932, 61–62)

The private language of this passage shows Bogan teetering on the edge between forced sanity and the reasonable un-reason that is coming over her. The conflicts were drowning her work. Somehow she managed to write in

1932 "a fine, frightfully angry, terrifically compressed poem . . ." (29 Nov. 1932, 69). Like "Henceforth, From the Mind," "Exhortation" was written as she hit bottom:

Exhortation

Give over seeking bastard joy
Nor cast for fortune's side-long look.
Indifference can be your toy;
The bitter heart can be your book.
(Its lesson torment never shook.)

In the cold heart, as on a page,
Spell out the gentle syllable
That puts short limit to your rage
And curdles the straight fire of hell,
Compassing all, so all is well.

Read how, though passion sets in storm
And grief's a comfort, and the young
Touch at the flint when it is warm,
It is the dead we live among,
The dead given motion, and a tongue.

The dead, long trained to cruel sport
And the crude gossip of the grave;
The dead, who pass in motley sort,
Whom sun nor sufferance can save.
Face them. They sneer. Do not be brave.

Know once for all: their snare is set
Even now; be sure their trap is laid;
And you will see your lifetime yet
Come to their terms, your plans unmade,—
and be belied, and be betrayed.

(67)

It is a poem like this that leads critics to write off Bogan as a "bitter" poet. She was aware of such a possibility: "Bitter though it be, do try to like it," she told her editor.[6] The active anger is perhaps healthier than the relative passivity of "Henceforth, From the Mind." Thirty years later she would explain that

> "Exhortation" and "Henceforth from the Mind" were written in my early thirties, in the midst of a state which bordered on despair. . . . The bitterness . . . is deepest in "Exhortation," which was written on the verge of a psychic and physical breakdown (which had roots in reality, and partook v. little of fantasy). (20 Aug. 1966, 368)

The poem may also be about a re-immersion in the literary scene of New York. The countryside had its advantages; not only did her husband have fewer temptations to infidelity, but they were away from the petty rivalries and jealousies that contaminate literary milieux. In 1930, thanking Harriet Monroe for a *Poetry* prize that would give her the courage to write again, Bogan spoke of the "creative despair" that had come about with the return to New York, and the reassertion of "a personal legend, that colored . . . opinion of my work." Being away, she had "forgotten the deadly persistence of rumor in a specialized group."[7] After several encounters where she was the subject of this "subtle and refined cruelty, I abjured poetry. I no longer wished to say myself" (24 Oct. 1930, 56–57). The five tightly constructed, rhymed stanzas of "Exhortation" quickly do away with "the dead we live among"; Bogan advocates indifference as the only stance against the world's cruelties, but it is an indifference that almost turns to Robert Frost's prescription for hatred. In the final stanza, she links the imagery of *Body of This Death* (snare, trap) and the thematic of *Dark Summer* (betrayal). In a sensitive review of *The Sleeping Fury* in 1937, Eda Lou Walton (one of the many women poets maligned by Bogan) wrote, "Betrayal has long been Miss Bogan's theme. At first it was the betrayal inevitable in love. Now this poet sees betrayal as common to all, as a betrayal of life itself."[8] I would add that there is a measure of deeply internalized self-betrayal in this determination not to "say oneself" when speech is the source of survival. These contradictory impulses—to speak and to be silent—would torment Bogan the rest of her life. On the one hand, she did want to bring up the emotional turmoil that was the stuff of her poetry because she was afraid she would go down with the memories. In her journal, she wrote that "the continuous turmoil in a disastrous childhood makes one so tired that 'Rest' becomes the word forever said by the self to the self. The incidents are so vivid and terrible that to remember them is inadequate; they must be forgotten." As William Maxwell sensitively pointed out, "the act of forgetting can be, of course, as difficult as the act of remembering."[9] This is precisely the precarious balance that marked Bogan's creative life.

It was no doubt cathartic for Bogan to write "Exhortation" but it also cut her off from others; this cannot be a permanent situation, for any person or any artist. In late 1932 Bogan was writing embarrassed little notes to friends asking them to recommend her for a Guggenheim. She hated asking for favors. This was her perfectionism again, her unwillingness to be an advocate for herself. For if she did her work and was *really good,* would she not be rewarded? She hoped to go to Europe; I suspect she felt she had to get some distance on her decision about Holden. She got the grant and left in April 1933, touring Italy, France and Salzburg, where "Faubourg," one of her attempts to write, was put to paper. Snatches of it are legible in the Amherst manuscripts, attesting to her utter misery: "Come to the edge of the city / And walk the three flights up . . . A thousand times in dreams / You've looked for such a home / Lost within a suburb / In an anonymous street / Where no one knows your name / And you know no men, either . . ." There she is "[h]idden within the flats / Nameless and without hope. . . ."[10] (The poet who loses the desire to say herself loses her name.) She was so miserable that she cut her trip short, and returned home to find her apartment re-arranged by her husband's latest girlfriend. She still could not bring herself to leave him. In November

1933 she experienced another breakdown. This time she resolved to continue treatment "until I'm good and cured" (JAR xxix). The poems of 1933 and 1934, "To Wine" and "At a Party," reflect the tremendous bitterness and hatred of this period. The Amherst manuscripts show a number of abandoned attempts to grapple with the Holden experience. The pain comes through in first lines and titles: "O early heard, framed for some brute delight"; "O figured forth in what we have lost and abjured"; "Oh come again, distilled through the blood"; "Old laugher of music, I hear you"; "O loved and nameless, with the last blood of my heart"; "Once held out fruitless hopes"; "One tree lifts, full in bud, and one is bare"; and "O thou so long dead."[11] The poems she did finish and publish are controlled: Bogan, in pain, is changing the female tradition. The reader is attracted to the terrific beauty of the poems and finds, underneath, the terror. "Short Summary," directly reminiscent of "Dark Summer" for its imagery of negation, captures with lyric intensity the emptiness and anger of endings. It is uncanny how Bogan speaks for Everywoman caught in heterosexual betrayal; and it is unprecedented in the female lyric tradition to express these feelings with such rigor and density. For example, what modern woman does not recognize the confrontation with a man's inability to look at himself, which Bogan bequeaths to us in "Man Alone":

Man Alone

It is yourself you seek
In a long rage,
Scanning through light and darkness
Mirrors, the page,

Where should reflected be
Those eyes and that thick hair,
That passionate look, that laughter.
You should appear

Within the book, or doubled,
Freed, in the silvered glass;
Into all other bodies
Yourself should pass.

The glass does not dissolve;
Like walls the mirrors stand;
The printed page gives back
Words by another hand.

And your infatuate eye
Meets not itself below:
Strangers lie in your arms
As I lie now.

(75)

The mirror image was always a compelling one for Bogan, reflecting as it does the attempt to see, to look; but the image in the mirror, with its own life (like a photograph) is not the thing itself, is always an interpretation. Reality is elusive. The mirror in "The Cupola" brings discovery and knowledge. Here, though, the man is so empty, so bereft of any distinguishing marks (except his infatuate eye) that he does not have even a reflection, or a symbol on a page. Men without an identity of their own seek life through women, woman after woman, in experiences of estrangement and alienation which they call love. Bogan's final lines, with the play on "lie," possess the power of truth. "I fought one fight—a crusade designed to make the man I loved tell the truth—for about five years, over and over again," she wrote (24 Jan. 1936, 124–25). But Holden was a chronic liar.[12] In this period of crisis, the poems were coming with great difficulty. Only seven were published between 1930 and 1934. Bogan had to choose either to leave the relationship or to go under with it. Here again we see the inextricable connection between Bogan's art and her life. She had always expected to be with a man; in "Second Act Curtain," the draft of a poem written in 1933, he was "earth and heaven" to her.[13] She was afraid to be alone. She also needed to write and to write was to confront her problems. On the one hand, her high standards demanded that poems come out of an unsparing, perfect emotional honesty. On the other, she felt she could not continue the exhausting struggle of knowing herself, and saying herself:

> Morton, I produced two poems, and sold them both for bread and shoes. I shall produce two or three more, if only to keep my promises to *Poetry* and to you. But thereafter the fountain will be sealed for good, I'm thinking. With Eliot, I pronounce poetry a mug's game (I called it a gull's game for years). I can no longer put on the 'lofty dissolute air' necessary for poetry's production; I cannot and will not suffer for it any longer. With detachment and sanity I shall, in the future, observe; if to fall to the ground with my material makes me a madwoman, I abjure the trade. Having definitely given up alcohol and romantic dreams, having excised my own neurosis with my own hand, having felt the knife of the perfectionist attitude in art and life at my throat. . . . But you can't stand this, I know.
>
> Forgive me for not being a female Dante. . . . (27 July 1934, 78–79)

When she wrote this, Bogan was back in New York after six months in a sanitarium—and she had left Holden. She is the mother who is responsible for the bread and shoes of herself and her seventeen-year-old daughter; she paid with her poems, "Man Alone" and "Short Summary." This is the woman-in-reality; and then there is the poet who thinks of herself in terms of Eliot of the mug's game (both *mug* and *gull* mean "one who is easily made a fool of") and Yeats of the "lofty dissolute air." She measures herself against these modernist masters and goes so far as to apologize for not being Dante, who produced an enormous corpus that makes her four or five poems seem insignificant indeed. The woman struggles to be woman and Poet (read "male") in line with the Western Tradition.

This letter haunted Tillie Olsen, who wrote of Bogan, in *Silences:*

> "The knife of the perfectionist attitude in art and life."

> This haunting sentence . . . is from *What the Woman Lived*, letters by the
> consummate poet, Louise Bogan—to me one of our most grievous 'hidden
> silences.' (Woman, economic, perfectionist causes—all inextricably inter-
> twined.)[14]

Louise Bogan is the paradigmatic modern woman poet, struggling to be
"perfect," having internalized male definitions of women's imperfections in
poetry and their ideas of what "perfect" is. The tension of being both
"woman" and "poet" resulted in breakdowns among many modern women
poets, H.D. and Millay among them; the struggles of Sara Teasdale finally led
to suicide. It is hard to face the fact that this has not changed much, although
in the present age we like to pretend that the woman artist can have it all. In
fact, it is more often the case that the woman artist (to paraphrase Yeats's
"The Choice") must choose between "perfection . . . of the work" and "the
heavenly mansion raging in the dark."[15]

Louise Bogan experienced terrible ups and downs during her lifetime. But
she did not give up. She was in fact terrified of being "the woman who died
without producing an *oeuvre*. The woman who ran away" (JAR 103). Somehow she kept re-finding the will to say: Her capacity for confrontation and
truth kept her art alive. After this particular siege, she started to bounce back,
in 1935. She published six poems in that year: "Poem in Prose," "To My
Brother," "Roman Fountain," "Rhyme," "Evening Star," and, to my mind,
one of her most beautiful "love" poems, "Italian Morning." Around this time,
thinking about the contents of a third book, she made a list of the poems she
had written and then made a note, "Ten others, and they must be as objective
as possible."[16] By objective, she does not mean impersonal but distanced, and
thus understanding of her situation. With "Putting to Sea," she got down and
through her agony with Holden. Her initial attempts to deal with the grief
yielded the kind of sentiments and language she had to keep working to
overcome. An early draft is laden with melodramatic speech ("It is Swamp-
scott, it is March, it is I . . . / Clouds, over the sea, motionless lie. / The sea is as
green as a turtle; as gray / as the iris of an eye . . . / Hither I came, soaked in
tears, twelve summers ago." Without objectification, the poem goes on to say
directly "I suffered" and "I sat soaked in my sorrow. . . ."[17] Bogan wanted to
render not the emotion itself but its effects; she accomplishes this in "Putting to
Sea" without saying directly "I have suffered." Known primarily for the short
lyric, the cri de coeur, which she preferred, she also seemed to need long-lined
free verse to work out certain kinds of grief. This poem uses the sea voyage as
metaphor for a plunge into self-knowledge; when we read it, we feel the echoes
of a long poetic tradition. In her version, Bogan is trying to exorcise the terrible
hatred that has supplanted love and, even more important for the women's
tradition, to face an unknown world that has no charts nor maps of expectation. "Who, in the dark, has cast the harbor chain?" the poem begins, dramati-
cally. The word "love" appears four times and is the reason for this voyage:

> Sodden with summer, stupid with its loves
> The country which we leave, and now this bare
> Circle of ocean which the heaven proves
> Deep as its height, and barren with despair.
>
> (BE 84)

In the midst of this empty scene, a voice calls, enticing the voyager to sensual experience. It is a decadent, destructive, and ugly sexual world that is called up here. Bogan was never one to shirk sexual imagery if it came up from the unconscious. In "The Changed Woman," in her first book, Bogan invoked male and female symbol, "Rocket and tree, and dome and bubble," as she wrote of the enticements and treacheries of love. There is the phallic imagery of "Roman Fountain" in *The Sleeping Fury,* the rendition of those "Great big bronze gents . . ." (2 July 1935, 91). Of "Musician," Bogan wrote to her former lover Theodore Roethke, "And that poem wasn't about music, idiot" (12 July 1937, 157). Its third stanza has "Now with great ease, and slow, / The thumb, the finger, the strong / Delicate hand plucks the long string it was born to know" (106). In "Putting to Sea" she is unsparing in her delineation of pleasure that has turned to disgust. The phallic imagery of "spiny fruits" and "coarse fruits . . . not fed by streams" is placed in contrast to a green time, dreamed of perhaps in youth; but now there is metal, "light obscene," and "flamy blooms," the horrific beauty of a symbolist landscape. The temptation is gotten through, though all that lies beyond are "sterile shores," a life that cannot be imaged, that is unknown. The poem ends in an act of courage, that she will persist

> And learn, with joy, the gulf, the vast, the deep.

This final line brings an unmistakable echo of Baudelaire in "Le Voyage":

> Plonger au fond du gouffre, Enfer ou Ciel, qu'importe?
> Au fond de l'Inconnu pour trouver *du nouveau!*
>
> To plunge to the depths of the abyss, Hell or Heaven, what
> does it matter? To the depths
> of the unknown in order to find the New![18]

Baudelaire's "new" refers both to sensations in the decadent sense but also to the new of the unconscious. For Bogan, "the gulf, the vast, the deep" is the unknown of a world she had not expected, that she is willing, after an interminable struggle, to face. For her, the poem signalled an ending. She wrote to her publisher of this poem (called at first "Goodbye at Sea") that it "will sum up the Holden suffering, endured so long, but now, at last completely over" ([June] 1936, 132). "I know what it's about, with my upper reason, just a little; it came from pretty far down, thank God" (29 July 1936, 133, n2).

Through therapy and poetry, she would go even farther down. What Bogan came to understand was that she brought her love-hate relationship with her mother into her heterosexual liaisons. In a draft of "Italian Morning," a poem about betrayed love (with its rejected phrases, "false coin," "false love," "in light counterfeited"), there is the image, also later abandoned, of the cutting of an apple: ". . . the rind / spiralling downward from the deft knife."[19] The image is startling because it reappears in a passage about her mother from her journal:

> My mother had true elegance of hand. She could cut an apple like no one else. Her large hands guided the knife; the peel fell in a long light curve down from the fruit. Then she cut a slice from the side. The apple lay on the saucer, beautifully fresh, white, dewed with faint juice. She gave it to me. She put the knife away. (JAR 27)

The last two sentences are masterly in their evocation of love and terror. In fact, Bogan now understood that she had come to like her patterns of perversity, that habit of sado-masochistic relation she had learned as a child and now transferred to adult relationships. A knowledge of these linkings came, for example, from one of the books on psychoanalysis recommended by her therapist. Bogan copied this passage into her journal:

> A grief-stricken person who has lost an object must loosen the libidinal attachment that binds him to it. This tie is not a matter of a single situation; the libido is attached to thousands of individual memories; and on each of the memories the dissolution of the tie must be carried through, *which takes time.* This process Freud designated the "grief work" (Trauerarbeit).[20]

Her journals provided one way of loosening the ties; poetry was another. In a second long poem, "The Sleeping Fury," Bogan brought together in a single powerful symbol her war with her mother and the child in herself. "The Sleeping Fury" is a forerunner of the many contemporary poems by women that speak of this most powerful relation. Bogan was one of the first to break the silence. The poem began with prose notes that convey a sense of the violence of the past and the fury as reconciler, "So that the girl could alter into the woman / Bearing her solitude."[21] Bogan brought into the final version as well this rage of the child, which had surfaced in "Summer Wish" (DS) but remained unresolved. This is, as Elizabeth Frank has pointed out, "the Child who lived within the adult Woman, locked away and silent, until forced by circumstances, betrayal, or time itself to disrupt, intrude, and clamor for recognition."[22] "The Sleeping Fury" begins in quiet:

> You are here now,
> Who were so loud and feared, in a symbol before me,
> Alone and asleep, and I at last look long upon you.

Your hair fallen on your cheek, no longer in the semblance of serpents
Lifted in the gale; your mouth, that shrieked so, silent.
You my scourge, my sister, lie asleep, like a child,
Who, after rage, for an hour quiet, sleeps out its tears.

(78)

With this scourge, this sister, this sado-masochistic relation, Bogan conflates all that obsessed her as an adult but that she had to relinquish in order to go on: her anger with her mother (her passion for her because she never had her), her dimly lit memories of violence between her parents, her own raging responses as a child. Here the child is a mother and the mother a child; here obsessions from the past are set apart, and understood. In the third stanza, Bogan's personal symbols from the unconscious are universalized. She rarely calls upon Greek myth in her poems but here she brings a depth and an irony to her discovery by invoking ancient origins. Moreover, she deepens the sense of female identity and connection by calling upon the Furies to promote revelation. The Fury is that force which, miraculously, mysteriously, pushes us to look at ourselves:

You who know what we love, but drive us to know it;
You with your whips and shrieks, bearer of truth and of solitude;
You who give, unlike men, to expiation your mercy.

The conflicts gotten through, the child in one both loved and relinquished, the fury has met its match:

Beautiful now as a child whose hair, wet with rage and tears
Clings to its face. And now I may look upon you,
Having once met your eyes. You lie in sleep and forget me,
Alone and strong in my peace, I look upon you in yours.

(78–79)

When the tumult and conflict is over, amazingly, we can hardly remember it, nor can it remember us. For the moment, Bogan felt strong, although alone: This was the victory of her "grief work." It was at this time that she wrote, "I am happy now—happy for the first time . . . I worked and fought for thirty-seven years, to gain serenity at thirty-eight. Now I have it . . ." (7 Oct. 1935, 109). Bogan often made such statements about something done with and completed; our lives do not know such full stops. Nothing is "over." Yet we often make such declarations about our lives when something has been gotten through; for Bogan, as for the rest of us, such declarations may give rise to expectations that cannot be met, may even prevent us from integrating our experience as we attempt to close the doors of the past.

Bogan's mother is the powerful presence that dominates "The Sleeping Fury": She was the woman who was hated for her defections but loved for her beauty and courage. The knowledge of the poem resides in its understanding that at some point we can no longer blame the past for our present; to be adult is to take responsibility for one's life. The same theme is sounded in "Kept":

> Time for the wood, the clay,
> The trumpery dolls, the toys
> Now to be put away:
> We are not girls and boys . . .
> (87)

There are echoes here of Sara Teasdale's 1931 poem, "In a Darkening Garden":

> Gather together, against the coming of night
>   All that we played with here,
> Toys and fruits, the quill from the sea-bird's flight,
>   The small flute, hollow and clear;
> The apple that was not eaten, the grapes untasted—
>   Let them be put away.
> They served for us, I would not have them wasted,
>   They lasted out our day.[23]

Bogan would surely have lopped off the last two lines of this poem had it been hers. The rendition is different yet the sentiment markedly similar, a legacy of the female tradition. What Teasdale wrote two years before her suicide, Bogan drew upon as she came to terms with the past in the middle of her life.

Several months after Bogan completed "The Sleeping Fury," her mother became ill. The first sentence of this letter refers to the curly-headed androgynous figure embossed on the cover of the original edition of *The Sleeping Fury*:

> The picture of the Fury came intact, and it is so beautiful that I cried. I would have written you before this, but my mother took sick the night before last, and today I managed to persuade her to go to the hospital, and it is pneumonia.

> If you could have seen the fight she put up, right to the last. But now she is a poor dying woman. I wish I could stop remembering her in her pride and beauty—in her arrogance, that I had to fight so—and now I feel it would have been better if I hadn't fought at all. Because under it all was so much love, and I had to fight that too. (To Morton D. Zabel, 23 Dec. 1936, 147)

Fight, fought: two fighting women. As a young girl, full of anger, who wanted fairness, as a child understands fairness, Bogan fought a mother who was full with anger. The struggle is elemental; in the poem, the speaker wants justice and vengeance. She learns there is no justice—only acceptance and love.

In fact, in 1935, Bogan was feeling confident enough to give herself to love again; she had an affair with Theodore Roethke and in 1937 began another, which lasted for eight years, with a man she met on a boat to Europe. "Song for a Lyre," placed at the very end of her third volume, is her beautiful paean to the possibilities of love. In 1935, too, she seemed to understand what she had sacrificed and she was prescient about the instability of calm. With "Evening-Star," she wrote one of her first "prayer" poems, not out of orthodox faith, but from a recognition in familiar rhythms of the vulnerability of our natures:

Evening-Star

Light from the planet Venus, soon to set,
Be with us.

Light, pure and round, without heat or shadow,
Held in the cirrus sky, at evening:
Accompany what we do.

Be with us;
Know our partial strength.
Serve us in your own way,
Brief planet, shining without burning.

Light, lacking words that might praise you;
Wanting and breeding sighs only.

(83)

The poem's dominant symbol of benevolence and peace is female, round, a goddess of love and beauty who shines but does not burn: The passion has been tempered. In the final stanza the poet points to her own immortal gift—for she has found words. One feels here a Bogan who is relinquishing some measure of control, giving in to a larger scheme of which she is a part. This acceptance brings temporary serenity. Yet she would continue that struggle with a nature that wanted more than life can give, that in its intensity could not find an easy place to *be,* since it was so drawn to giving in to passive resignation or giving up entirely.

As she prepared her third book for publication, Bogan looked back on what she had been through, what she had weathered. Blessed again with a certain calm and resolution, she was able to depict with humor those difficult years:

The S.F. is now in sections: four of them. It rises and falls, from despair to exaltation, and back again. Bogan in cothurnus and Bogan in flat heels. "S. for a Lyre" . . . is the last poem in the book, and I want it set in italics, to give M. Rukeyser, K. Patchen, S. Burnshaw, H. Gregory and M. Zaturenska something *really* to worry about. 'Miss Bogan ends on a typical note of feminine love, as might be expected. In her next we no doubt will get the let-down from her latest emotional spree. If we are alive when her next appears . . .' (They won't be, I hope.)

Seriously, the poems shape up pretty well. The 1930–33 period—despair, neurosis and alcoholism—is set off by itself, ending with "Hypocrite Swift." Then the spiritual side begins, with a few rumbles from the sensual bassoons and the mystic fiddles. All ends on a note of calm: me and the landscape clasped in each other's arms. (To Morton D. Zabel, 8 Dec. 1936, 145)

Bogan felt that "Song for a Lyre" was the best love poem she had ever written, "perhaps the only love poem I ever wrote" (14 Nov. 1936, 142). She is right that she has given the critics what they expected from a woman poet: a book of torment that ends in love. A book ending with Nature and the Poet "clasped in each other's arms" places Bogan firmly within the romantic tradition; at the same time, *The Sleeping Fury* redefines modernist themes as it insists on the value of female experience. The modernist aesthetic decrees that Poetry must reflect suffering and a fascination with what is difficult. For Louise Bogan knowledge came through love and brought hard-won self-acceptance.

VIII.

"THIS LIGHT IS LOSS BACKWARD"
POEMS AND NEW POEMS (1941)
AND COLLECTED POEMS 1923–1952
(1954)

> Feeling requires strength.
>
> —Marina Cvataeva

> Now from the south I gaze with sanity
> extreme . . .
>
> —Louise Bogan

Between 1937 and 1941, when her first collected poems came out, Bogan wrote fourteen new poems. She was against the collection. Her perfectionism spoke again: "Poor Scribner's is making another attempt to impress me upon an unwilling public," she wrote to Theodore Roethke (Sept. 1938, 182–83, n1). She finally gave in to the plan for *Poems and New Poems:*

> I enclose the signed contract. I can't understand why Scribner's is doing this, and I'm against the book, on principle. Mark Van Doren's *Collected Poems* has just come in, and again I say: 'What earthly good does it do?'—I shall endeavor, however, to write a series of Dinggedichte for you. Can you suggest any subjects? The Zoo has been rather overdone, perhaps. I might write an Ode to the Passing of the Sixth Avenue Elevated, on whose platforms I have shed many a tear. . . . (To John Hall Wheelock, 29 Jan. 1939, 182)

Bogan did not like losing her sense of dignity to the demands of the market-place; yet it was not crass financial motive that moved her publisher, John Hall Wheelock, to put out another book. He believed in Bogan's talent and wanted to keep her name before the public. The collection did not appear until 1941, not a particularly good moment to re-introduce Louise Bogan. Bogan's reference to *Ding-Gedichte,* "object poems," is in part jest, in part a reflection of her attempt to try out new kinds of poems. *Ding-Gedichte* is a term coined by Rilke, who looked hard at objects or animals in order to get "inside" them.

121

Thus parts IV and V of *The Blue Estuaries* (which is the *Poems and New Poems* section) includes Marianne Moore-like excursions ("Animal, Vegetable and Mineral," "Variations on a Sentence"); four- and even two-line observations; a long-lined, prosy, and sarcastic rendition of an "Evening in the Sanitarium" and translations, including "Kapuzinerberg" and "From Heine." Bogan did not think that this a book made. Most of the new poems were written in 1937 and 1938; besides these almost occasional poems, there are some magnificently inspired ones. For Bogan was relatively happy in 1937: She had a new book out, she headed off to Ireland to resume her "Gugg." On that trip, she began the successful and secretive love affair with the Irish-American electrician she met on board ship. This was the man who "says *Nuttin* when he means *Nothing;* his parents come from Sligo," the county where Yeats's mother had grown up and where Yeats spent much of his first ten years. As William Maxwell tells us, "Though she mentioned him to her friends, she did not allow any of them to meet him."[1] Out of this relationship came a trio of truly lovely poems, poems that, unlike some of the more forced experiments of *Poems and New Poems,* are pure Bogan. Of "To Be Sung on the Water," whose "s" and "o" and "p" sounds imitate the sound of moving through water quietly, with slightly lapping oars, Bogan wrote: "I'm going right back to pure music: the Christina Rossetti of our day, only not so good. My aim is to sound so pure and so liquid that travelers will take me across the desert with them . . ." ([Sept.] 1937, 163). Two other poems, "Music" and "Cartography," represent love in an uncomplicated, direct manner that is unusual in the Bogan oeuvre. "Music" is pure sensuality, "Cartography" evocative of the way erotic love puts us in touch with all that we do not know, those mysteries that are beyond rational comprehension. Only in "Come, Sleep . . ." is there a reminder of the insomnia that plagues the lover who is at once "selfish devourer" and "selfless lover" (108). Love is woman's subject, and it was Bogan's subject "par excellence." With these poems she tapped the source once again.

With "The Dream," Bogan brings again the confrontation with demons, this time in a narrative mode that is much lighter in tone than the long meditations of *The Sleeping Fury.* Twenty-five years later, Bogan said of the poem:

> "The Dream" is a later poem, written in my late thirties after a complete change in my way of living, and in my general point of view about life (and the universe at large!). It is the actual transcript of "a nightmare," but there is reconciliation involved with the fright and horror. It is through the possibility of such reconciliations that we, I believe, manage to live. (20 Aug. 1966, 368)

"Reconciliation" is the key word here. Bogan felt this was "a poem of victory and release. The terrible power, which may v. well be the psychic demon, is tamed and placated but *not* destroyed; the halter and the bit were already there, and something was done about control and understanding" (14 Aug. 1954, 369, n1). The demon cannot be completely destroyed, for this is the stuff of art. Madness, after all, she realized in 1939 after she had been through it, has its function: "Madness and aberration are not only parts of the whole tremendous set-up, but also, I have come to believe, *important* parts. Life trying new ways out and around and through . . . all the horrors must Mean Something . . ." (19 Jan. 1939, 180–81). Yet "The Dream" has less intensity than many of her confrontation poems. It feels like a rendition of the fear once the fear is over; the earlier poems give us the feeling as it is being felt. The poem's structure, its story-telling mode, contribute to this effect. Bogan, resolved, reconciled, was simply less intense. Reconciliation, resignation, acceptance—each of the expressions points to a giving up, perhaps even an underlying depression.

In "The Daemon," first published in April 1938, she asks again, as she had after her second breakdown, whether she can keep calling up the experience that is the basis of her art:

The Daemon

Must I tell again
In the words I know
For the ears of men
The flesh, the blow?

Must I show outright
The bruise in the side,
The halt in the night,
And how death cried?

Must I speak to the
Lot who little bore?
It said *Why not?*
It said *Once more.*

(114)

To pose the question is to indicate a waning of poetic desire and energy. Now, in her forties, having been through so much, Bogan was trying to keep a kind of terrible balance. In the past, it was partly her femininity she feared she would lose if she kept pursuing art. Now, she did not want emotion to get out of hand because she was less willing to give up her sanity for art. She knew that to keep the cap too tightly on emotion would prevent poetry; and, paradoxically, it was poetry that somehow kept her alive. Her perfect understanding of this precarious balance was expressed later in her life, in a 1958 review of the autobiography of Caitlin Thomas, the widow of Dylan Thomas:

Innocence and violence are terrible things. The severe rituals imposed on adolescents in practically every tribe known to anthropology insist on two basic dicta: *Grow up* and *Calm down*. In maturity, it is necessary, mankind has discovered, to suppress outbursts of strong emotion—joy, rage, grief—that may, in their irrationality, disturb the general peace. . . . Yet it is true, and always has been, that innocence of heart and violence of feeling are necessary in any kind of superior achievement; the arts cannot exist without them. (PA 387–88)

The conjunction of innocence and violence is striking, given Bogan's child-hood. If you let emotion get out of hand, you may go under; if you do too much growing up and calming down, you will lose art. Bogan had to find the precarious midpoint that made art out of emotion but which did not go too far toward flooding. In a moving retrospective essay, May Sarton, who had learned this from Bogan, charted the terrible balance:

> Her detachment, what seemed sometimes "unkind," was part of her armor, necessary for survival. One must see her spotlighted against a terrifying darkness that was always there in the background and that, at least three times in her life, required hospitalization. It took me a long time before I understood how carefully she must design each day to keep the demon at bay, how carefully she must balance any emotional expenditure against possible disaster.[2]

This demon is the catalyst both for the "perfect" poetry coming from a deep emotional source—the only kind of poetry Bogan wanted to write—and the originator of breakdown. May Sarton passed on what she had learned from Bogan about the precarious balance of the woman artist. She has the heroine of *Mrs. Stevens Hears the Mermaids Singing* say, "Women are afraid of their demon, want to control it, make it sensible like themselves." Carolyn Heil-brun, quoting this passage, immediately thinks of Bogan's criticism of "Women," who "have no wilderness in them" and "are provident instead." "Wildernesses are not tidy," Heilbrun knowingly remarks.[3]

By 1940, when she wrote "Zone," Bogan felt the off-again, on-again depres-sion coming on again. She often felt depressed in March, during the palest light of the year. The first draft of "March Twilight" dates from this period; a revised version of the poem would appear in her last collection. Of "Zone," Bogan would later write:

> In the late 30's, in a transitional period both of my outer circumstances and my central beliefs, I wrote a poem—"Zone"—which derives directly from emotional crisis, as, I feel, a lyric must. And I think that the poem's imagery manages to express, in concrete terms (the concrete terms which poetry demands), some reflection of those relentless universal laws under which we live—which we must not only accept but in some manner forgive—as well as the fact of the human courage and faith necessary to that acceptance. (JAR 118)

Bogan's perfectionism, solidified almost into rigidity, is reflected in this pas-sage written in 1962. The reconciliation had begun many years before, as Louise Bogan sought to relinquish expectation, to be patient, to wait. After her second breakdown, she had copied out from Jung's *Psychology of the Uncon-scious* a passage that describes maturity as "the building up of a personality . . . adapted to reality, *who does willingly* and without complaint everything required by necessity" [Bogan's emphasis].[4] It is this theme of acceptance, emerging in "The Dream," which informs "Zone." She would bear up under depression, recognizing it as familiar, knowing, or at least hoping, it would pass. Bogan's new patience, which bordered on resignation, was beginning to affect her work.

It was in 1941, with the appearance of the *Poems and New Poems* that she had so opposed, that Marianne Moore wrote a review characterizing Bogan's work as "compactness compacted." ("Women are not noted for terseness, but Louise Bogan's art is compactness compacted.")[5] At that point, too, Malcolm Cowley, full of admiration for Bogan's perfect oeuvre and aware that her "theory of art" made it "difficult or impossible to write a great deal," wrote:

> *Poems and New Poems* is not a big volume, but it contains everything that Miss Bogan thinks worth saving from her work of the last twenty years. . . . Other poets publish more in a single season. Even quantitatively, however, Miss Bogan has done something that has been achieved by very few of her contemporaries; she has added a dozen or more to our small stock of memorable lyrics. She has added nothing whatever to our inexhaustible store of trash.
>
> Nevertheless, I hope she now decides to make some change in her theory and practice of the poet's art. Together they have been confining her to a somewhat narrow range of expression. Her new poems—meditative, witty and sometimes really wise—suggest that she has more to say than can be crowded into any group of lyrics; and that perhaps she should give herself more space and less time. Most American poets write too much and too easily; Miss Bogan ought to write more and more quickly.[6]

Bogan was probably depressed by such reviews; Cowley's advice was sound—but she could not take it. It was contrary to all she had imagined for her art. Many notices took Cowley's point of view; Louise Bogan had written well but should write more. Others, like Babette Deutsch, praised the work but criticized the publication of a padded collected poems that added little to the oeuvre.[7] Bogan had been afraid that this book would mar her perfect work. There was, of course, much to take heart from in the reviews, but an artist as self-critical as Bogan probably focused on the negative comments. In 1941, still resisting the collection, she had written to her editor, "I am so out of the general line now; and I really have been so battered about that I don't care any more. What good does it do?" (24 Feb., 215). The verb "battered" is striking, given her experience of abuse in childhood, the last line a repetition of the misgivings she had expressed in the letter to Wheelock quoted at the beginning of this chapter. Marie Collins conjectures that "Bogan's sense of being 'unknown' " was simply fortified by the 1941 collection.[8] Not having a sense of an audience is devastating for a writer. And the injunction to write more was probably understood by her as a lack of appreciation, a misunderstanding of her aesthetic.

There were no poems between 1941 and 1949. Bogan was very busy in the forties; "unknown," she was still reaping the rewards of a certain success, giving lectures at universities, moving briefly to Washington to serve as Consultant in Poetry to the Library of Congress, sitting on awards committees. And, of course, she was still writing those endless reviews for the *New Yorker*. This job undermined Bogan's creative life; writing to Katharine S. White of the

New Yorker in 1948 as she tried to work on her journals, she said, poignantly and insightfully: "Criticism, when practiced over years, makes the creative side rather timid" (14 Oct. 1948, 262). This burden, her precarious psychological balance, her perfectionism, her sense of being unappreciated, and her idea of the innate limitations of the woman poet now combined to effectively put an end to her art in her early forties. For those of us who have traversed Bogan's career in these chapters, this end is no surprise; one way to analyze her early silence is to realize that she had predicted as much. She set it up, in this way, in her mind: This is, quite simply, prophecy fulfilling itself. "Women collapse so thoroughly, so soon," she had written after meeting Willa Cather in 1932 (29 April 1932, 65).[9]

Had she not, in her coup de grâce of Millay in 1939 (the very year her publisher began to suggest a collection) written that, "it is difficult to say what a woman poet should concern herself with as she grows older, because women poets who have produced an impressively bulky body of work are few" (PA 299). That is, if woman's traditional subject is love, then what was a woman to write about when love was over? Surely this idea of limitation had something to do with the traditional tragic view of the brief, brilliant life of inspiration of the lyric poet:

> Apprenticeship, a period of full flowering, and a gradual decline in creative energy—the usual progress of a lyric poet who does not force or falsify his gifts. (JAR 121)

Bogan believed in poetic "gift" and its necessary decline. Such an idea was especially deadly for women. Yet her definitions of female lyric limitation reflected prejudices current in her time. Here is Bogan's good friend, Edmund Wilson, writing about a woman artist, a novelist, in this case, whom he defines in terms of limitation:

> When we look back on Mrs. Wharton's career, it seems that everything that is valuable in her work lies within a quite sharply delimited area—between *The House of Mirth* and *The Age of Innocence*. It is sometimes true of women writers—less often, I believe, of men—that a manifestation of something like genius may be stimulated by some exceptional emotional strain, but will disappear when the stimulus has passed. With a man, his professional, his artisan's life is likely to persist and evolve as a partially independent organism through the vicissitudes of his emotional experience. Henry James in a virtual vacuum continued to possess and develop his métier up to his very last years. But Mrs. Wharton had no métier in this sense. . . .[10]

Ironically enough, this is from an article called "Justice to Edith Wharton." It is Roethke's idea of women's artistic limitations, albeit in a slightly different form. Women's art depends on great emotion; we cannot write to order, in the distanced way men can (and this capacity is a virtue, according to Wilson). Men's subject matter is broader, larger, includes politics, history, culture, religion, which they control. We are opposite. Bogan learned this idea of the difference between women and men, and women and men's art, from the culture and from her male friends. She internalized it completely. Wilson delivered his judgment of Edith Wharton in 1937, the same year *The Sleeping Fury* came out, dedicated to him "in gratitude." Bogan repeated Roethke's declarations about the limitations of the woman poet in her 1962 talk at Bennington. Hers, then, was an aesthetic of limitation, demanded by her temperament and her age, which was lying in wait to condemn the woman poet for her sentimentality, her effusions, her lack of range—a lack of range at once deplored and named as natural.

Two poems Bogan would re-find and rewrite in the fifties issue from this period and indicate that she was very discouraged in the early forties. On 1 April 1940 she wrote to a friend that she had "sold the 'March' poem, and . . . written another called 'The Sorcerer's Daughter.' Have also started in to translate Supervielle . . ." (206). "March Twilight" (127), first written on 1 March 1940, brings some insight into what Bogan was feeling at the beginning of that decade when she wrote so little. That inspired line which would open the poem was more deeply buried in the 1940 version:

> Suddenly upon the edge of day and of the season
> Events occur a little above themselves, as out of time;
> A little which way, a little altered for an inscrutable reason,
> Like the pentatonic scale half resolved in the normal, or an off-rhyme.

> This light is loss backward; delight by hurt and by bias gained
> Nothing we know about and heightened all-that-we-shan't have.
> It is light which easily might have shone upon our birth
> And presages our grave.[11]

Even in this first draft, Bogan represses the outward events in order to capture the emotions they inspire. How the hurt came, whether through professional strains (as in "Exhortation") or through painful love, is not the issue for poetry, in her view. In the version rewritten in the fifties, Bogan changes the second stanza to the first and makes the March light central, dropping the more obscure metaphor. These changes render a more powerful generalization about life's unfairness. There are only minor changes in the first two lines of the second stanza ("youngest" becomes "newest" and "The light" "light"). The last two lines of the poem were altered to create a substantial change in tone and effect. The 1940 version reads:

> The shipwrecked in these new late beams might well find one other face
> And look into its eyes, as into a strange house, for what lies within.

The final version has

> A watcher in these new, late beams might well see another face
> And look into Time's eye, as into a strange house, for what lies within.
>
> (127)

Bogan gives the final version more distance as the drama of "the shipwrecked" is changed to the observation of "a watcher." With Time, she says what she had meant with the death image in the original poem but now she says it more abstractly, less personally. In this way, she makes the poem an expression of existential anguish and of the human condition, whose disillusionments give way to a coming to terms with death.

"The Sorcerer's Daughter" makes more explicit the feelings that had emerged in the early version of "March Twilight." Bogan was beginning to feel unlucky: "It was crossed from the start / With all the marks of luck changing from better to worse. / And by these tokens I begin to think it is mine" (125). This is a new theme in the work of a poet who had emphasized personal responsibility, the capacity to take control, through strength, of one's destiny. Her translation of Jules Supervielle's "To the Unknown" dates from this period, with these notes ". . . addressing a word to Thee / My God" appearing in her papers:

> I who do not even know if you exist
> And do not understand the language of your whispering churches,
>
> I do not believe in thee, but I wish to speak to you all the same . . .[12]

More and more, as the years went on, Bogan would turn to poems in the prayer mode. Inspired by them, she would write her own versions of an appeal for peace.

In 1946, after four years of poetic silence, Bogan wrote a letter to Rolphe Humphries (noted in the first chapter) in which she expressed satisfaction with the state of her bank account and her good health but lamented that she could not "self-start" anymore, that the "daemon has been silenced" and that, after all, there was "so little time left, before decay sets in" (7 Oct. 1947, 254–55). In 1948 she finally met true inspiration in the person of T. S. Eliot. ("I sat beside the Great Man at lunch; and I looked into his Golden Eye. How beautiful is the combination of physical beauty (even in slight decay), high qualities of mind and heart, and *perfect humility*" (28 Nov. 1948, 265). Out of it came the extraordinarily beautiful, and poignantly titled, "Song for the Last Act," a tribute to the immortality of art. Rolphe Humphries helped Bogan with the stanzaic arrangement and she was jubilant, grateful:

> I want to thank you for your *great help*. Katharine White of *The New Yorker* took the poem with great glee; so at least one more poetic work will be published proving that *women* can carry on to some slight degree, in their 50's. (1 Jan. 1949, 267, n1)

Bogan had an extraordinary sense of her poetic mission; she still feels responsible for advancing the women's tradition. But the Muse visited seldom and without the strength of earlier inspirations. A poem published in a small magazine three years later illustrates this lack of force:

The Catalpa Tree

Words do not come to the old prayer,—only the rung names and the pauses.
An autumn I remember only by the pods of the catalpa tree that did not fall.
Tears were shed, sobbed to wild herbs in a field, whatever their causes,
And a house had a wall like a web of thorns about it. I remember that wall.

Only the long pods remained; the tree was drained like a sieve.
Perhaps the secret voice you hear under your mouth was all I could keep:
The burnished pods not claimed by a wizened month once said I should live.
They hang in my song of another autumn, in this hour stolen from sleep.[13]

It is rather amazing that Bogan published "The Catalpa Tree." The poem evokes others we have read—the negation (pods that do not fall), the tears, a house that walls one in. It is as though Bogan were writing from the memory of her past poems. The yoking together of the prayer and the song modes is surely unconscious yet a striking insight. Bogan was still stealing hours from sleep to try to write; and in the same year inspiration broke through again. In 1951 she published two more lovely poems, her highly original "Train Tune," evocative of an older woman looking back, with love, upon her experience, and "After the Persian," a further meditation on the question "Why write?" which was posed in "The Daemon" in 1938. In fact, the two poems are placed opposite each other in her final volume. In the earlier poem, the persona decides, albeit grudgingly, to drag out the feelings again in order to continue speech; in "After the Persian" the response is one of a fifty-four-year-old woman who is tired of tumult:

I

I do not wish to know
The depths of your terrible jungle . . .

I am the dweller on the temperate threshold . . .

(115)

In the second section of the poem, the speaker remembers the passions of her youth, and its devastations. The section ends with the startling image of her eight-sided heart. The line is explicable only with Bogan's gloss on it, in a letter to May Sarton in 1954:

As for my eight-sided heart, which you question, dear May, I can only say that the octagonal here is somehow symbolic of freedom. Love of things, I suppose, understood, more than love of human beings. . . . The delight in objects, both natural and artifacts, which has grown in me ever since the *obsessive* person was left behind (or buried, if you like, in the lowest layer of the dream). The delight of the collector, which you sensed in my room; the delight of the naturalist (which I never had, when young, except in flashes, but which makes me scrutinize everything, from flowers to rocks on the shore, in these later years); the delight of the amateur in the arts (the piano and embroidery); the delight of

the cook and the housewife. . . . All these are substitutes, I know; but they keep
me alive and not only happy but occasionally full of joy. I do not speak of the
delight of the maker, for writing has never been anything (except v. rarely) but
tough and artisan to me. (4 Feb. 1954, 283–84)

These are not unlike the sentiments of renunciation of "Henceforth, From the
Mind," published in 1931. Now, criticism seemed to help her feel that she was
productive. *Achievement in American Poetry, 1900–1950,* written quickly,
was published in 1951. As a poet, she did not feel free to pursue the subjects
that Yeats, for example, permitted himself—laments about aging, the sexual
fantasies of an old man. Self-pity was one of the emotions she did not admit to
her poetry. Yeats's pathos borders on self-pity, perhaps, but his lamentations
are real, and moving:

> What shall I do with this absurdity—
> O heart, O troubled heart—this caricature,
> Decrepit age that has been tied to me
> As to a dog's tail?
>
> ("The Tower")

> You think it horrible that lust and rage
> Should dance attention upon my old age;
> They were not such a plague when I was young;
> What else have I to spur me into song?
>
> ("The Spur")[14]

Yeats names his sources of inspiration and keeps writing. Bogan was not alone
among the women poets of her generation who felt they could not as women
write of how they felt about the aging of their bodies, or being alone, or the
growing and leaving of their children. Only in the contemporary period have
women poets felt so free.

To Art as subject Bogan continued to bring consummate expression. In
Section II of "After the Persian" she pays tribute to her accomplishments as an
artist:

> All has been translated into treasure

and this, one of her loveliest lines, is followed by a parting that, because it is so
beautiful, seems almost premature. Here there is the luxuriousness and the
melancholy of the Eastern poems which in part inspired her words:

> IV

> Ignorant, I took up my burden in the wilderness.
> Wise with great wisdom, I shall lay it down upon flowers.

V

Goodbye, goodbye!
There was so much love, I could not love it all;
I could not love it enough.

Some things I overlooked, and some I could not find.
Let the crystal clasp them
When you drink your wine, in autumn.

(117)

Collected Poems, 1923–1953 was published in 1954, adding "After the Persian," "Train Tune," and "Song for the Last Act" to the poems of the 1941 collection. Marie Collins notes that "what perhaps is surprising is that Bogan was so well known, after so long a silence."[15] Léonie Adams wrote a long and thoughtful review of the collection, and Elder Olsen, a professor of English at the University of Chicago, offered what is perhaps the first piece of serious criticism. John Ciardi was cute about her youthful work; in a review of Bogan, Adams, and Millay entitled "Two Nuns and a Strolling Player," he noted that Adams and Bogan had once been "sisters in the same aesthetic convent" ("I must confess that I have often wondered why that sisterhood insisted on wearing its chastity belts on the outside. . . .") as he announced his preference for the more mature work, when "Miss Bogan leaves the convent" to wrestle with real-life demons. Her later work, he says, is "timeless."[16] (Does he mean sex-less?) The review is a mix of praise undercut by his rejection of her earlier, female, subject matter; it is a little incredible that a fifty-seven-year-old respected poet still had to read such notices. More important, as Collins has pointed out, is that Bogan was being discovered by younger poets such as Richard Eberhart. There is no sign, however, that young women writing in the fifties opened Louise Bogan's books to discover what she had to teach them.

IX.

"NOW I AM NOT SURE"
THE BLUE ESTUARIES: POEMS 1923–1968 (1968)

> Listen to me. I want to tell you something
> very important. All of writing is a huge
> lake. There are great rivers that feed the
> lake, like Tolstoy and Dostoevsky. And
> there are trickles, like Jean Rhys. All that
> matters is feeding the lake. I don't matter.
> The lake matters. You must keep feeding
> the lake. It is very important. Nothing else
> is important.
>
> —Jean Rhys

Louise Bogan's manuscripts at Amherst reveal many poems begun but unfinished, many lines started but not pursued. In the fifties, she was looking for things to publish and found some old poems. In 1957 she wrote to her old friend and former publisher from Scribner's:

> This year I recovered two older first drafts—one from the summer of 1955, and one going back at least 15 years—and *carpentered* them up, and sold them. Their titles are rather old-fashioned: one is called "July Dawn" and the other "March Twilight." (To John Hall Wheelock, 16 Feb. 1957, 308)

Here is both her sense of thrill with craft and her assessment, which increased over the years, that she is out of the general line. "July Dawn," symbolizing "dis-hope," was published in a special folio edition in San Francisco along with her final "manifeste," much calmer in tone than "The Springs of Poetry" (but still depending on the male pronoun). Bogan says again that the lyric gift has always been recognized as "chancy and unreliable," that it "comes and goes" and that "a poet can never be certain, after writing one poem that he will ever be able to write another." The poet cannot even count on his craft because "the 'breath,' the 'inspiration' may be gone forever." She continues:

> All one can do is try to remain "open" and hope to remain sincere. Openness and sincerity will protect the poet from giving in to fits of temper; from small emotions with which poetry should not, and cannot deal; as well as from

imitations of himself or others. The interval between poems, as poets have
testified down the ages, is a lonely time. But then, if the poet is lucky and in a
state of grace, a new emotion forms, and a new poem begins, and all is, for the
moment, well.[1]

This is Bogan's perfect perfectionism manifest at the age of sixty; her allusion
to breath and inspiration are evocative of the romantic aesthetic, her references
to luck and grace particularly poignant seen in the context of the forties poems.
In 1959 Bogan found another poem, "The Sorcerer's Daughter," which we
have discussed, written twenty years before, and added to it "a set of lyric
notes" called "The Young Mage," which (as she told a new young friend) she
published at the request of the *Times Literary Supplement* (To Robert Phelps,
3 Nov. 1958, 317). "The Young Mage" has the fluency and musicality of
many of her earlier poems even if its meaning is elusive: Almost didactic, it
advises what to enjoy, and what to avoid, in order to survive. But it is also as
though we are being told of life's mystery and magic, the difficulty of interpret-
ing the signs that come to us.

With "The Sleeping Fury," Bogan had added to her themes of love and art
what I have called her confrontation poems, a mode that came out of therapy
and from her more conscious understanding of the unconscious. In 1957 she
added another poem to this group. In contrast to "The Sleeping Fury" and "A
Dream," there is in "The Meeting" no reconciliation to be found:

The Meeting

For years I thought I knew, at the bottom of the dream,
Who spoke but to say farewell,
Whose smile dissolved, after his first words
Gentle and plausible.

Each time I found him, it was always the same:
Recognition and surprise,
And then the silence, after the first words,
And the shifting of the eyes.

Then the moment when he had nothing to say
And only smiled again,
But this time toward a place beyond me, where I could not stay—
No world of men.

Now I am not sure. Who are you? Who have you been?
Why do our paths cross?
At the deepest bottom of the dream you are let in,
A symbol of loss.

Eye to eye we look, and we greet each other
Like friends from the same land.
Bitter compliance! Like a faithless brother
You take and drop my hand.

(129)

Less rigorous stylistically than her earlier work, this poem is nonetheless pure
Bogan in its brutal honesty. It is amazing to be able to admit at the age of sixty

that one does not understand all one thought one had understood. Is not age, with all its loss, at least supposed to bring sagacity? Peace and reconciliation fly out the window in such moments of terrible uncertainty. Taken literally, this man could be the spectre of her second husband emerging again—both May Sarton and Sylvie Pasche indicate that she kept loving him to the end. But, seen symbolically, the poem is surely meant to represent the way that, just when we think we have put something behind us, it returns to haunt us again. Bogan had been startled into this perception more than once; in 1954, for example, she found a packet of letters her husband had written in 1933 and lived through the pain, once again (JAR 125–26). The poem is "about" our meeting with any demon with which we think we have contended. Bogan's own gloss on the poem confirms this view; she first thought she would do it in prose and then "it came out practically whole, although a few shifts had to be made. The change in the dream-creature's personality had taken place; the creature started out being Raymond at his most guileful, of course. And I always thought of the locale at the bottom of the dream" (15 Mar. 1957, 309).

In the early sixties, there were three poems that came from observation rather than from tumultuous emotional experience—"St. Christopher," "The Dragonfly," and "Morning." I do not find these *Ding-Gedichte* as compelling as Bogan's lyric poems but clearly it was important for her to work on them: These efforts kept the creative urge alive. They may very well have made possible the re-emergence of eloquence, once again. In 1962, in her sixty-fifth year, Louise Bogan wrote her finest late lyric. "Night" also brought with it the title for her last volume of poems.

Night

The cold remote islands
And the blue estuaries
Where what breathes, breathes
The restless wind of the inlets,
And what drinks, drinks
The incoming tide;

Where shell and weed
Wait upon the salt wash of the sea,
And the clear nights of stars
Swing their lights westward
To set behind the land;

Where the pulse clinging to the rocks
Renews itself forever;
Where, again on cloudless nights,
The water reflects
The firmament's partial setting;

—O remember
In your narrowing dark hours
That more things move
Than blood in the heart.

(130)

"Night," like "Zone," is a poem about "those relentless universal laws" Bogan had acquiesced to for some time; we remember her view, expressed in the thirties, about the inevitable stream and flow of history that we cannot, as individuals, paw out of shape. This was an idea that grew in meaning as she grew older. "Night" begins descriptively, almost matter-of-factly; yet we can feel in these rhythms a building up through metaphor that will bring, finally, a larger statement, a statement that again harks back to romantic belief. That sense of nature's continuity and renewal and permanence is the accomplishment of the third stanza; and in the last, the human is placed in relation to Nature. We are a part of Nature and, as a part, we are not more significant than the whole. Bogan had given up the comforts of orthodox religion and traditional philosophy years ago. But, human, she was afraid of being nothing. In her journal she had asked herself: ". . . What am I afraid of / Death?—for one thing yes—that is part of it."[2] "Night" is an attempt to allay the fear, and the hubris.

Some of these later poems, and "Night" is one of them, are more accessible than Bogan's earlier work. When she did write in her later years, she seemed to speak more simply, more directly. This sense of accessibility comes in part from the subject matter, the "universal" confrontation conveyed in the later poems. After "Night" in *The Blue Estuaries* Bogan placed "Morning," one of her *Ding-Gedichte,* which brings a much less intense and sober treatment of the theme of nature's renewal, and even wiseness. In "Night" I see the sure hand of an accomplished artist with the repetition of the "o" sounds in the first and the ultimate stanza; its dirge-like rhythm; and its images from nature whose force—that which moves us deeply—comes from simplicity, an elegant simplicity that is won only from skill, and living.

In 1967 Bogan sent three "songs" to the poetry editor of the *New Yorker;* they seemed to her "to belong to the same world (of dream and aberration)" (25 Jan. 1967, 371). "Psychiatrist's Song" and "Little Lobelia's Song" were written in the winter of 1966–67; "Masked Woman's Song" was "a fairly old erotic song" dating from 1940 (372, n2).[3] "Psychiatrist's Song" was originally titled with a "recitative" spoken by the clinician followed by the patient's "aria." These divisions are not preserved in the final poem although it is clear there are two speakers. Hauntingly enough, the poem is an echo of her previous work: Bogan returns to the imagery of decadence and the metaphor of a journey that she had used in "Putting to Sea." Here she does a play on "man" (mango, mangrove, mandrake); here the temporary peace is found through mother earth. The end of the poem is strongly reminiscent of the "goodbye" of "After the Persian":

> Farewell, phantoms of flesh and of ocean!
> Vision of earth
> Heal and receive me.
>
> (135)

This is the first time we hear echoes of past work in Bogan's oeuvre, a way of saying both "all has been translated into treasure" and "I have said it all, I am repeating myself." And repetition, for Bogan, was prohibition. Had she not warned against—in her 'ars poetica' accompanying "July Dawn"—the poet who imitates himself or others?

In a compelling little essay called "Circumscriptions" Ruth Limmer thinks through the reasons for Bogan's near silence after 1940. She notes how in the letters Bogan's "is the voice of restraint," that "even at the furthest end of her tether, she is in absolute control: the walls of the permissible are not breached" (171).[4] Limmer believes, with many of us, that Bogan's reticence is a relief in an age of unbridled confessionalism; she sees its drawbacks as well. Bogan refused to be a public poet, to make available to critics and newspapermen the details of her personal life. This reticence "alienated the larger audience which . . . wants access to its poets" (171). More important, this reticence "had the effect of circumscribing her talent" (171). Limmer says she knows of nothing in the forties that Bogan would want to hide—and surely the poet has given us the personal in her poems, hiding neither her capacity for drink nor for sado-masochistic relation, though she has given it in the most veiled forms possible. By the time she reached forty, Bogan had so closely defined what one can write about and what one cannot, that she had "hemmed in" her talent and effectively "put a stop to her own freedom. This far, she said, no further" (172). Limmer believes that "her strictures kept her from the range of expression that many men, neither more nor less talented, have been able to achieve" (172). And finally,

> In the course of working through this essay, I have come to entertain the possibility that the grief and frustration that absorbed her last years may have had their origin in her chosen circumscriptions; and that what I will continue to call dignity, taste, and a belief in the (qualified) sacredness of art—*but which may also be called a fear of revealing oneself*—kept her from full creative freedom. (172)

Bogan kept up the fight to write, to reveal somewhat, until the early forties. "But then something happened. Call that something the impact of life itself, for which one pays; call it the overburdening demands for renunciation, and control; call it cumulative silence" (173). I think all of these are important. That Bogan had suffered immensely, as a woman and as a poet, we have seen in these chapters; her utter exhaustion would be reason enough for effectively putting an early end to her creative work. To the renunciation in her work— and to this pattern of renunciation as it pervades women's poetry—we have also alluded. As for the control, it came out of Bogan's temperament and from the milieu. Modernism prescribed control; there was an additional burden for the woman poet who had to show that she could overcome the female poetic tradition. As for "cumulative silence," we have seen that Bogan's output was always sparse; she renounced poetry more than once only to return to it. Thus it is not utterly unexpected that these silences would end in a final, early silence.

Limmer ends her essay with a reference to one of Bogan's last poems, "Little Lobelia's Song." This was written (as we noted in the first chapter) when the poet was valiantly fighting off the effects of Librium, which gave her brief relief from depression and then brought on fits of weeping. The poem went through several revisions, the major one a change from direct speech ("Let me back to sleep / But don't let me die / Though I weep, weep / Though I cry, cry") to the fashioning of a child-like alter ego, "Little Lobelia," who brings back the ghosts the poet thought she had laid to rest. For Limmer, this song ("I know nothing / I can barely speak") is emblematic of Bogan's circumscriptions, which she puts in the context of the female poetic tradition:

> Had Bogan not so severely limited the scope of female expression—if she had allowed women the license she permitted to men—might little Lobelia have sung a somewhat less despairing song? We cannot know. But it is a question to explore as we ponder, for our own purposes, the dialogue between the woman poet's life and her art. (174)

As early as 1923, at the age of twenty-six, in "The Springs of Poetry," Bogan had articulated an aesthetic that would almost inevitably lead to silence. It was there, as we remember, that she said the poet should write through "clenched teeth," that he must "subsidize his emotion by every trick and pretense so that it trickle out through other channels, if it not be essential to speech." In this early statement of the nature of poetry, she had called upon the poet, whom she imaged as male, to inhabit "a stern countryside that could claim him completely, identify him rigidly as its own. . . ."[5] It is as though, in an act of defiance, she had taken the modernist aesthetic to its extreme in order to disprove what she had also internalized from the culture, the notion that women poets could not control their emotions. Bogan, because of these intertwining interdictions, finally achieved such control that she could no longer express any emotion at all.

CONCLUSION
REDEFINING LITERARY MODERNISM

> Let a woman learn in silence with all sub-
> missiveness. I permit no woman to teach or
> to have authority over men; she is to keep
> silent.
>
> —1 Tim. 2:11–12

> The deepest feeling always shows itself in
> silence;
> Not in silence, but restraint.
>
> —Marianne Moore

> Women have not only been mute—they
> have tried to *conceal* (through clothes,
> language).
>
> —Meridel LeSueur

> My head is full of whispers which tomor-
> row will be silent.
>
> —Adrienne Rich

> And I hear even my own voice becoming a
> pale strident whisper.
>
> —Audre Lorde

Louise Bogan's narrow definition of modernism contributed to her silence; this
was a definition not only of her making but a woman poet's response to her
milieu. Because of her gender, she narrowed the prevailing definitions of
modernism even further. The subordinate often takes the rules literally. Bogan
knew intuitively what we can now see from the vantage point of historical
distance. Modernism—or that highly selective modernism dominant in her
time—was in fact hostile to "feminine" qualities. Modernist critical perspectives began to be developed in the twenties and thirties; T. S. Eliot's
criticism and reviews by poets and journalists were the precursors of the
academic New Criticism. To read reviews by some men of women poets in the

twenties and thirties is to experience the onset of an extreme "anti-feminine" reaction.[1] That is, those qualities which these reviewers traditionally associated with women, such as openness and emotional warmth, were declared not adequate for poetry; by this definition, then, no woman could ever write poetry that passed the modernist test.[2]

In 1920, as Louise Bogan began to take herself seriously as a poet, the female vote had been won; "sexual liberation" had become the new myth of the urban white middle class; World War I, heralded as apocalypse, ended in catastrophe, as wars only can. Out of this historical context developed a critical and creative hegemony that can be seen as a triumph of scientism and masculinism in its most extreme forms, a triumph that lasted until the fifties when "confessionalism" released emotion again.

Louise Bogan could be extremely lucid about the battle lines marking the speech permitted to women and men. In 1938, a year before the publication of her last complete volume, she was able to say of the state of poetry: "The whole lyrical school now began to suffer an eclipse. . . . When unmixed with new hardness and vigor, its forms dropped into limpness or its emotion receded into bathos. Female lyric grief came in for some ridicule and not a little contempt."[3] The sexual metaphor is obvious, the ambivalence pure Bogan. This study has shown how she at once subscribed to and recreated the selective modernism that reigned as she was trying to establish herself as a poet. Her intelligence created an original response to two traditions, a brilliant, if momentary, female redefinition of those contending claims.

Louise Bogan's tiny oeuvre and her early silence can be linked, then, to a woman's adherence to a selective modernism and to her further narrowing of that tradition. Her silence is quite different from the silence of a Valéry or the aesthetic of silence of late modernism. For Samuel Beckett, for example, and for some other male modernists who comprise the canon as we have understood it, silence is a reflection of existential angst, the expression of nothingness through the extinction of language. For Bogan, on the other hand, and perhaps for many other "minority" writers as well, silence is a form of self-censorship and the subordinate's drive to perfection. With these writers, it is more accurate to speak not of *silence* but of *silencing*, in the sense of being silenced by the culture and by internal constrictions.[4] It is, of course, ironic that, having become more perfect than perfect, Louise Bogan is still ignored.

A study of Louise Bogan, or any other female modernist, has broad implications. Clearly, what has been called "modernism" in the academy is, in fact, a modernism dominated by a few figures. Women poets have been either left out entirely or at best rendered marginal to Canonical High Modernism, which has spoken primarily of the white tradition and the heterosexual one. The New Criticism, while valuable for its instruction in close readings of the text, left out white women and the literary expressions of women and men of color and the art of lesbians and homosexuals; in a concomitant move, it left out "politics," or a consideration of the social context of the artwork. In fact, those poets esteemed as the Major Modernists (Yeats, Eliot, Stevens, Pound) are much more complicated, much more interesting, much more "personal," than the dominant critical tradition would have us believe. Literary modernism, in short, was flattened by New Critical approaches, and now it is being allowed to billow out into all its contradiction and complexity.[5]

Our re-interpretations must offer new evaluations of the Masters—including considerations of their political conservatism—as it opens the field to those poets who disagreed with their conservative views. Female modernism, that recasting of the tradition achieved by Louise Bogan and others, is only beginning to be defined.[6] It means the experimental work of writers such as Gertrude Stein and H.D., who left the United States to find artistic freedom; it includes the very different poetry of Louise Bogan, a female romantic modernist; and it must take into account the poems of the women of the Harlem Renaissance.[7] As we at once create a new canon and question the very idea of one, we need to be aware of what we are putting in, and what we are leaving out.

Louise Bogan's "aesthetic of limitation" was the conscious strategy of a woman poet who wanted to be put in; up to now, she is proof of the "no-win" position of the modernist woman poet.[8] Until we expand our definitions of literary modernism she, and others, will be left out; moreover, as long as poetry is enacted and evaluated within a dominant white male paradigm, all the "others" will perform contortions of suppression and expression like those I have underlined in this book.

NOTES

In citing works in the notes, short titles have been used. Full particulars are given in the bibliography. Page numbers given for poems quoted in the text refer to *The Blue Estuaries* unless otherwise indicated. Citations of *Critical Essays* refer to *Critical Essays on Louise Bogan*, edited by Marie Collins. The following abbreviations have been used in text and notes for frequently cited works by Bogan.

AA   *Achievement in American Poetry, 1900–1950*
BD   *Body of This Death*
JAR   *Journey Around My Room: The Autobiography of Louise Bogan, A Mosaic*
PA   *A Poet's Alphabet: Reflections on the Literary Art and Vocation*
WWL   *What the Woman Lived: Selected Letters of Louise Bogan, 1920–1970*

The epigraphs before the Contents page are taken from "I might have sung of the world," *Mirror of the Heart: Poems of Sara Teasdale,* ed. and intro. William Drake (New York: Macmillan, 1984), xlix, and *Silences* (New York: Delacorte Press/Seymour Lawrence, 1965), 145.

Introduction: The Aesthetic of Limitation

Epigraphs: Bogan, JAR 120. Cheryl Walker, *The Nightingale's Burden: Women Poets and American Culture before 1900* (Bloomington: Indiana University Press, 1982), 20. Lola Ridge, " 'Woman and the Creative Will': A Lecture by Lola Ridge," ed. Elaine Sproat, *Michigan Occasional Papers in Women's Studies* 28 (1981), 2.

1. See my review of contemporary Bogan criticism, "The Pursuit of Perfection," *Women's Review of Books,* July 1985, 8–9.
2. Tillie Olsen, *Silences,* 145.
3. Cheryl Walker's point is in her Ph.D. dissertation, "The Women's Tradition in Poetry," Brandeis University, 1973, 214–15. Mary de Shazer's analysis is included in her paper, "My Scourge, My Sister: The Silent Muse of Louise Bogan," delivered at a conference on women's poetry at Stanford University, 1982. A revised version of the paper is published in *Coming to Light: American Women Poets in the Twentieth Century,* ed. Diane Wood Middlebrook and Marilyn Yalom (Ann Arbor: University of Michigan Press, 1985). "Women" was printed separately for private distribution by the Ward Ritchie Press of Pasadena in 1929. Elizabeth Frank speculates that "Bogan may have been thinking about another poem," Lizette Woodworth Reese's "Women." Reese's poem was published in *White April and Other Poems* (New York: Farrar & Rinehart Winston, 1930), 8; she lived from 1856 to 1935. Her "Women" also offers a catalogue of our shortcomings:

> Some women herd such little things—a box
> Oval and glossy, in its gilt and red,
> Or squares of satin, or a high, dark bed—
> But when love comes, they drive to it all their flocks;
> Yield up their crooks; take little; gain for fold
> And pasture each a small forgotten grave.

When they are gone, then lesser women crave
And squander their sad hoards; their shepherd's gold.
Some gather life like faggots in a wood,
And crouch its blaze, without a thought at all
Past warming their pinched selves to the last spark.
And women as a whole are swift and good,
In humor scarce, their measure being small;
They plunge and leap, yet somehow miss the mark.

See *Louise Bogan: A Portrait* (New York: Alfred A. Knopf, 1985), 65–67.

I. Outlines of an Artist's Life

Epigraph: La Rochefoucauld quoted in Louise Bogan, "From the Journals of a Poet," *New Yorker*, 30 Jan. 1978, 39.

1. Ibid.
2. In a letter to John Peale Bishop on the latest gossip, including news of Elinor Wylie's connubial bliss and Edna Millay's marriage, Wilson wrote: "I may close this department of my intelligence by noting that Raymond Holden has heroically left his wife and family and is now living in sin with Louise Bogan—a third lady poet of remarkable achievement . . . Raymond is trying to get a divorce and marry her. If he succeeds in doing so, all the remarkable women of the kind in New York will be married to amiable mediocrities. I do not know whether this is a very unfortunate thing or a very beneficial and reassuring one" (Edmund Wilson, *Letters on Literature and Politics, 1912–72*, ed. Elena Wilson [New York: Farrar, Straus, & Giroux, 1957], 118). Wilson's comments are not disinterested—he was always half in love with Bogan himself. And he usually had a wife to take care of him.
3. Elizabeth Frank, in her biography, *Louise Bogan: A Portrait* (New York: Knopf, 1985), presents a balanced picture of the Bogan-Holden marriage; she does not attempt to place blame but shows how each partner contributed to the failure of the relationship. She notes that Holden's subsequent life appears to have been considerably less tortured than Bogan's. See p. 287.
4. Wilson, *Letters*, 234.
5. William Maxwell, "Louise Bogan's Story," review of *Louise Bogan: A Portrait* by Elizabeth Frank, *New Yorker*, 29 July 1985, 76.
6. Ibid.
7. Frank, *Portrait*, 285–86.
8. Ibid., 286.
9. May Sarton, "Louise Bogan," *A World of Light* (New York: W. W. Norton, 1976), 228.
10. Richard Hughes and Robert Brewin, *The Tranquilizing of America* (New York: Warner Books, 1979), 36.
11. Ibid., 299.
12. Ibid., 5. Heart palpitations are also a symptom of anxiety and often associated with nervous breakdown.
13. Frank, *Portrait*, 397.
14. Elizabeth Roget (pen name of Sylvie Pasche), personal conversation, 6 Feb. 1982, Bolinas, California.
15. Ibid.
16. Sarton, *World of Light*, 233.

II. The Authority of Male Tradition

Epigraphs: T. S. Eliot, "Tradition and the Individual Talent," *Selected Prose of T. S. Eliot,* ed. Frank Kermode (New York: Harcourt Brace Jovanovich, 1975), 38. Kermode notes that Eliot "maintained that his early criticism achieved its success partly because of its dogmatic manner and because it was, inexplicitly, a defense of the poetic practice of his friends and himself" (11). Laura Riding and Robert Graves, *A Survey of Modernist Poetry* (London: William Heinemann, 1929), 155. Woolf quoted in Tucker Farley, "For Whose Eye?," review of *The Diaries of Virginia Woolf,* Vol. 5, 1936–41, ed. Anne Olivier Bell, *Women's Review of Books,* July 1985, 16. Farley's review opens with this passage: " 'I have been thinking about Censors. How visionary figures admonish us . . . If I say this So & So will think me sentimental. If that . . . will think me bourgeois.' So Virginia Stephen Woolf muses in the recently published fifth volume of her diaries. Wordsworth didn't have censors, she continues, so his poetry was not restless but beautiful and still, undistracted, 'As if the mind must be allowed to settle undisturbed over the object in order to secrete the pearl.' " Florence Howe, "Introduction," *No More Masks!: An Anthology of Poems by Women,* ed. Florence Howe and Ellen Bass (Garden City, N.Y.: Doubleday Anchor, 1973), 7. I am deeply indebted to this book for my introduction to women's poetry.

1. Louise Bogan, "The Situation in American Writing: Seven Questions," *Partisan Review* 6 (1939), 105. The questionnaire is reprinted in *Critical Essays,* 49–53.
2. Ibid., 105.
3. Ibid.
4. Arthur Symons, *The Symbolist Movement in Literature* (New York: E. P. Dutton, 1958), 66–67.
5. Ralph Freedman, "Modern Poetics," *Princeton Encyclopedia of Poetry and Poetics,* ed. Alex Preminger (Princeton: Princeton University Press, 1965), 512.
6. Jaqueline Ridgeway, *Louise Bogan* (Boston: Twayne Publishers, 1984), 15. The letter is in F. 2, New York City Library, Berg Collection, May Sarton Letters.
7. Stéphane Mallarmé, "Les Fenêtres," *Mallarmé,* trans. Anthony Hartley (Baltimore: Penguin, 1965), 18. Translation mine.
8. Freedman, "Modern Poetics," 512.
9. In 1929, with the publication of *Dark Summer,* Bogan wrote to her publisher, John Hall Wheelock, asking him to send her books to Maine's State Library, adding that "I'll send them a picture of my birthplace, which will strike them dumb, I am sure. The house has *such* a cupola and eaves made of gingerbread, and in the picture's foreground my mother is holding me, an infant of six months, of extremely simple appearance, in her arms" (13 Nov. 1929, 50).
10. *Mallarmé,* ix.
11. May Sarton, *Journal of a Solitude* (New York: W. W. Norton, 1973), 130. Jean Dominique is the pen name of Marie Closset.
12. Roger Williams, *The Horror of Life* (Chicago: University of Chicago Press, 1980).
13. For example, in 1933, in the midst of a severe depression and feeling especially cut off, she wrote in her journal: "At the newsreel theatre—I said to myself: Very well, why should I not let down and become part of this? How ridiculous I am here, in my isolation and my half-elegance . . . Let down—believe—be part of it. O disordered, meaningless life. Let down. But I could not" (JAR 84). She got through the depression and wrote the poems of reconciliation and acceptance that would form *The Sleeping Fury.*
14. Frank J. Warnke, "Metaphysical Poetry," *Princeton Encyclopedia of Poetry and Poetics,* 495.

15. T. S. Eliot, "The Metaphysical Poets," *Selected Prose,* 60.

16. Louise Bogan, "To a Dead Lover," *Poetry* 20 (1922), 250–51.

17. Jeanne Kammer, "The Art of Silence and the Forms of Women's Poetry," *Shakespeare's Sisters: Feminist Essays on Women Poets,* ed. Sandra M. Gilbert and Susan Gubar (Bloomington: Indiana University Press, 1979), 158.

18. Susan Schweik's work unburies these responses. See "A Word No Man Can Say for Us: American Women Writers and the Second World War," Ph.D. diss., Yale University, 1984.

19. *Mirror of the Heart,* xix.

20. The lines are from Rilke's "Der Schauende" ("The Spectator") in *Buch der Bilder.*

21. W. B. Yeats, quoted by William Drake, *Sara Teasdale, Woman and Poet* (New York: Harper & Row, 1979), 121–22.

22. Bogan, "The Situation in American Writing," 107.

23. *Selected Poems and Two Plays of William Butler Yeats,* ed. and intro., M. L. Rosenthal (New York: Macmillan, 1963), xxvii. Edward Engelberg argues that "through the assertion of a single image" Yeats found that vastness could become as intense and focal as a lyric system." This assuaged his disappointment that he did not live in an epic age. See *The Vast Design: W. B. Yeats's Aesthetic* (Toronto: University of Toronto Press, 1964), 4.

24. Harold Bloom, jacket notes, *Louise Bogan Reads from Her Own Works,* Yale Series of Recorded Poets, Decca, DL 9132. Reprinted in *Critical Essays,* 85.

25. Sandra Gilbert and Susan Gubar, *The Madwoman in the Attic: The Woman Writer and the Nineteenth Century Literary Imagination* (New Haven: Yale University Press, 1979), 48.

III. The Female Heritage: Ambivalence and Re-vision

Epigraphs: Marya Zaturenska, letter to the author, 28 Nov. 1976. Louise Bogan, "Verse," *New Yorker,* 21 Oct. 1944, 94. Léonie Adams, letter to the author, 13 Dec. 1976. Amy Lowell, "The Sisters," *No More Masks!* 40–44.

1. Theodore Roethke, "The Poetry of Louise Bogan," *Selected Prose of Theodore Roethke,* ed. Ralph J. Mills, Jr. (Seattle: University of Washington Press, 1965), 133–34. Of course, such ideas were common at the height of Bogan's poetic career. In 1935, describing The Question of the Woman Poet for her anthology of verse, one editor quoted another on women's qualities and deficiencies: "Sheer sensitivity to bodied or unbodied stimuli, intimacy of treatment, patience with form, tenderness and tact with small things, and ability to see in small things terrific things, pronounced spirituality, and emotional maturity." On the negative side: "Sentimentality, narrow scope, over-subjectivism, vanity, preoccupation with self in a kind of bright egotism, lack of cosmic sense and lack of historical sense." This no-win catalogue was compiled by Virginia Moore for an essay on women poets in the *Bookman,* July 1930, and quoted by Tooni Gordi in her introduction to *Contemporary American Women Poets,* "Issued under the Auspices of The Spinners: A Bi-Monthly of Women's Verse" (New York: Henry Harrison, Poetry Publisher, 1936). Gordi sifted through 30,000 poems by 3,000 women for her collection. She published Bogan's "For a Marriage."

2. Bogan wrote to Rolphe Humphries: "Just at present, having snuck out of the center of the whirlwind, I'm taking a nice nap, and polishing my fingernails at its edge. No one can stay alive very long in the mood out of which I wrote you that letter. While the storm still yelled around I wrote telling the Taggard-Wolfs good-bye forever—and it's broken them all up, I guess. They are fond of me and I of them. Their fondness this morning took the shape of two letters, in which they called both Raymond and myself

habitual drunkards and reminded me that I probably would fill a dipso's grave because it was in the blood. It may be cruel to them, but I've got to be my own kind of damn fool, and not anybody else's kind . . ." (28 Aug. 1924, 13–14). A letter to Edmund Wilson commented on Taggard's poem: "Genevieve's book [*Not Mine to Finish*] came to hand the other day: in one poem she takes me to task for being a mocker and a fritterer; I sat down and composed the enclosed work after reading her opus. She's really very talented, but she is *so* transparent. The new gag is being and becoming a second Emily Dickinson: the Taggards came from Amherst after all, it would appear! O God save us all from harm and danger!" (16 Oct. 1934, 81–82). Taggard's biography of Dickinson had appeared in 1930. Her poem came out in *Not Mine to Finish: Poems 1908–1934* (New York: Harper & Brothers, 1934), 29.

3. The poem is reprinted in the letters, p. 82. It was the inspiration for the economical and intense four-line version, "To an Artist, to Take Heart."

4. I have been unable to find any indication that Bogan or other white women poets knew the black women who were active in the Harlem Renaissance in the twenties. The only references to black people in the letters are to rather exotic beings from whom she feels a distance, with whom she does not have any real, friendly contact.

5. Elaine Showalter, ed., *These Modern Women* (Old Westbury, N.Y.: Feminist Press, 1978), 3.

6. Ibid., 63. Showalter says this comment appeared in Taggard's *Collected Poems;* I have not found it in the first edition.

7. Léonie Adams, quoted by William Jay Smith, "Louise Bogan: A Woman's Words," *The Streaks of the Tulip* (New York: Delacorte, 1972), 45–46. Subsequent references to this talk will be indicated by page number.

8. In a letter to the author, 13 Dec. 1976.

9. Ann Stanford, ed. and intro., *The Women Poets in English* (New York: McGraw-Hill, 1972), xxxvii.

10. Letter, 13 Dec. 1976.

11. Louise Bogan, "Poetesses in the Parlor," *New Yorker,* 5 Dec. 1936, 42. Quotations that follow are from this essay.

12. Walker, *The Nightingale's Burden.* See especially "Conclusion: The Mythical Nineteenth Century and Its Heritage."

13. Rufus Griswold, ed., *Female Poets of America* (Philadelphia: Parry and McMillan, 1859), 7.

14. Allan Ross Macdougall, ed., *Letters of Edna St. Vincent Millay* (New York: Harper, 1952), 173.

15. Louise Bogan, review of *Conversation at Midnight,* by Edna St. Vincent Millay, *New Yorker,* 7 Aug. 1937, 51–53.

16. Anne Cheney, *Millay in Greenwich Village* (Fayetteville: University of Arkansas Press, 1975), 74.

17. For a detailed discussion of some of Millay's war poetry and of the vicious male critical response to it, see Susan Schweik's "A Word No Man Can Say for Us: American Women Writers and the Second World War," Ph.D. diss., Yale University, 1984, 76–83.

18. Sharon Mayer Libera, "Maine Remembered," review of *Collected Poems* by Edna St. Vincent Millay, *Parnassus* (Fall/Winter 1976), 210.

19. Wendy Martin's term in *An American Triptych: Anne Bradstreet, Emily Dickinson, Adrienne Rich* (Chapel Hill: University of North Carolina, 1984), 10. Martin writes that "traditionally . . . the jeremiad, political speech, and literary epic are male forms requiring a command of public space that women have not had."

20. Cheney, *Millay,* 132.

21. T. S. Eliot, "Tradition and the Individual Talent," *Selected Prose of T. S. Eliot,* ed. Frank Kermode (New York: Harcourt Brace Jovanovich, 1975), 43.

22. Bogan, "The Situation in American Writing," 105.

23. Genevieve Taggard, *The Life and Mind of Emily Dickinson* (New York: Knopf, 1930), xi.

24. Bogan may have seen the 1890, 1891, or 1896 editions or *The Single Hound, Poems of a Lifetime,* published in 1914. The 1924 edition edited by Bianchi and Hampson was re-issued in 1926 and *Further Poems* published in 1929. In *Achievement in American Poetry* Bogan particularly notes the 1924 edition. See p. 80.

25. Gilbert and Gubar, *Madwoman,* 591.

26. Bogan, "The Situation in American Writing," 105.

27. Horace Gregory and Marya Zaturenska, *A History of American Poetry 1900–1940* (New York: Harcourt Brace, 1942), 277.

28. Sarton, *World of Light,* 217.

29. Louise Bogan, "Verses," *New Yorker,* 21 Oct. 1944, 94.

30. Marianne Moore, letter to H.D., 29 Oct. 1944, Beinecke collection, Yale University.

31. Barbara Guest, *H.D.: The Self Defined* (New York: Doubleday, 1984), 133. There is no mention of Bogan in Guest's biography of H.D.

32. Louise Bogan, review of *Tribute to Angels* by H. D., *New Yorker,* 29 Dec. 1945, 68.

33. Louise Bogan, review of *The Flowering of the Rod* by H.D., *New Yorker,* 14 Dec. 1946, 147.

34. Elizabeth Frank writes that Sara Teasdale invited Bogan to tea in 1930 but Bogan was too depressed after the Hillsdale fire to take up the invitation (*Portrait,* 133).

35. Diane Wood Middlebrook traces this heritage in "Limits of Willpower: Louise Bogan's 'The Alchemist' " in her *Worlds Into Words: Understanding Modern Poems* (New York: W. W. Norton, 1978), 58–63.

36. She had read, for example: "One must face the fact that the opinions of Church Fathers, whose ideas replaced the teachings of Christ, appear to have been for women as dismal as they were unfortunate. For men, on the contrary, the Church, like Islam, carried much that was advantageous, for Christendom and Islam made available emotions, states of mind and political conditions by which men could profit, in which they could revel, and through which power could be won and justified" (Charles Seltman, *Woman in Antiquity* [London: Thames and Hudson, 1956], 198).

37. Bogan might almost have been thinking of herself when she writes of Richardson:

> Well, there you have her—in part: the brave little wrong-headed-to-the-majority partisan of her own sex, in her high-necked blouse and long skirt, from which the dust and mud of the London streets must be brushed daily; working long hours in the poor light at a job which involves physical drudgery as well as endless tact (she was a fashionable dentist's assistant); going home to a tiny bedroom under the roof of a badly run boardinghouse; meeting, in spite of her handicapped position, an astonishing range of kinds of human beings; going to lectures; listening to debates at the Fabian Society (of which she became a member); daring to go into a restaurant late at night, driven by cold and exhaustion, to order a roll, butter, and a cup of cocoa; trying to write, truthfully and as a woman; loving her friends, her country week-ends, her London. And continually sensing transition; welcoming change; eager to bring on the future. And reiterating: "Until it had been clearly explained that men were always partly wrong in their ideas, life would be full of poison and secret bitterness."

38. Lowell, 40–44.

Part II. The Achievement

Epigraphs: Hope Anderson, review of *The Journals of Sylvia Plath, Womennews,* San Francisco Commission on Women, Sept. 1982, 8. Laura Riding, "Preface," *Selected Poems in Five Sets* (New York: W. W. Norton, 1973), 12–13.

IV. "Epitaph for a Romantic Woman": Early and Uncollected Poems and *Body of This Death* (1923)

Epigraphs: Ridgeway, *Bogan,* 25–26. "The Betrothal of King Cophetua" was originally published in the *Boston University Beacon,* April 1918, 298. Louise Bogan, "The Young Wife," *Others* 4 (1917), 13.

    1. Margaret Homans, *Women Writers and Poetic Identity* (Princeton: Princeton University Press, 1980), 8.
    2. Ridgeway, *Bogan,* 24–25. Ridgeway points out that Bogan tries to give her poem psychological motivation.
    3. Ridgeway, *Bogan,* 25–26. Ellen Moers wrote about this metaphor, noting Freud's comments on the subject: "I run down Freud's list . . . of those things which in dreams symbolize the female genitals: boxes, chests, pockets, ships, churches and stop at the jewel-case, because of George Eliot." See *Literary Women* (New York: Doubleday, 1976), 252–56. It is quite possible that the young Bogan read *Middlemarch* and *Daniel Deronda* as part of her high school training.
    4. Rachel Blau DuPlessis, "Romantic Thralldom in H.D.," *Contemporary Literature* 20 (1970), 178–79.
    5. Bogan, "The Young Wife," 11–13.
    6. For example, see Rachel M. Brownstein's *Becoming a Heroine: Reading About Women in Novels* (New York: Viking, 1982).
    7. Jaqueline C. Ridgeway, "The Poetry of Louise Bogan," Ph.D. diss., University of California, Riverside, 1977, 37. "A Night in Summer" was originally published in *Jabberwock,* a publication of The Girls Latin School in Boston, 1913 (?). A clipping of the poem is in Folder 45 of the Bogan Papers in the Amherst College library.
    8. Louise Bogan, "Survival," *Measure* 9 (Nov. 1921), 5.
    9. Louise Bogan, "Elders," *Poetry* 5 (1922), 248. Here is the poem in its entirety:

Elders

At night the moon shakes the bright dice of the water;
And the elders, their flower light as broken snow upon the bush,
Repeat the circle of the moon.

Within the month
Black fruit breaks from the white flower.
The black-wheeled berries turn
Weighing the boughs over the road.
There is no harvest.

Heavy to withering, the black wheels bend
Ripe for the mouths of chance lovers,
Or birds.

Twigs show again in the quick cleavage of season and season.
The elders sag over the powdery road-bank,
As though they bore, and it were too much,
The seed of the year beyond the year.

10. Bogan, "Resolve," *Poetry 5*, 248–49. Elizabeth Frank thinks this poem registers the experience of Bogan's affair with John Coffey, an Irishman who stole fur coats to call attention to the plight of the poor (*Portrait*, 44–45).

11. William Drake gives the date of this poem as 1911. See his edition of Teasdale's poetry, *Mirror of the Heart*, 5.

12. Bogan, "Leave-taking," *Poetry 5*, 250.

13. Bogan, "To a Dead Lover," *Poetry 5*, 250–51.

Epigraph on p. 76: In his introduction to Moore's *Selected Poems* published in 1935, Eliot defends her choice of subject matter: "For a mind of such agility, and for a sensibility so reticent, the minor subject, such as a pleasant little sand-coloured skipping animal, may be the best release for the major emotions. Only the pedantic literalist could consider the subject-matter to be trivia; the triviality is in himself. We all have to choose whatever subject-matter allows us the most powerful and most secret release; and that is a personal affair. The result is often something that the majority will call frigid; for feeling in one's one way, however intensely, is likely to look like frigidity to those who can only feel in accepted ways." This sensitive introduction is re-published in *Marianne Moore: A Collection of Critical Essays,* ed. Charles Tomlinson (Englewood Cliffs, N.J.: Prentice-Hall, 1969), 63.

14. The poem from *Body of This Death* (New York: Robert McBride & Co., 1923), 2, reads:

Decoration

A macaw preens upon a branch outspread
With jewelry of seed. He's deaf and mute.
The sky behind him splits like gorgeous fruit
And claw-like leaves clutch light till it has bled.
The raw diagonal bounty of his wings
Scrapes on the eye color too chafed. He beats
A flattered tail out against gauzy heats;
He has the frustrate look of cheated kings.
And all the simple evening passes by:
A gillyflower spans its little height
And lovers with their mouths press out their grief.
The bird fans wide his striped regality
Prismatic, while against a sky breath-white
A crystal tree lets fall a crystal leaf.

Suppressed poems quoted in the text are from this edition. Other page numbers refer to the final collection, *The Blue Estuaries*.

15. *Webster's New World Dictionary,* Second College Edition, 1978.

16. And in fact she knew parts of it by heart. In 1937, piano-shopping with Maidie, what she played "ad lib" were "the chords which presage, in P[élleas] and M[élisande], the downfall of M's hair" (To Morton D. Zabel, 9 Oct. 1937, 164).

17. Homans, *Women Writers and Poetic Identity,* 216. Homans writes that "language is inherently fictive and creates masks whether or not the speaker or writer wishes it" and that "it is chasing phantoms to expect that language will suddenly work for the expression of women's truth. This aim is fundamentally antithetical to the aims of poetry . . ."

18. Carolyn Burke, "Review Essay. Supposed Persons: Modernist Poetry and the Female Subject," *Feminist Studies* 11.1 (1985), 136.

19. Cheryl Walker, *The Nightingale's Burden,* 30.

20. Frank, *Portrait,* 61.

21. I am indebted to Jaqueline Ridgeway for this version from the Douay Bible, which Bogan probably read in Catholic school. *Paul's Epistle to the Romans,* 7:21–24, Printers of the Holy See, 1899 is quoted in *Bogan,* 32.

22. Frank, *Portrait,* 54–55. Arthur Symons's essay on Mallarmé is in *The Symbolist Movement in Literature* (New York: E. P. Dutton, 1958), 70.

23. A. Donald Douglas, review of *Body of This Death, New Republic,* 5 Dec. 1923, 20, 22.

24. Mark Van Doren, review of *Body of This Death, Nation* 117 (1923), 494.

V. Interlude: "The Springs of Poetry" (1923)

Epigraph: T. S. Eliot, *Selected Essays* (New York: Harcourt Brace, 1932), 9.

1. Louise Bogan, "The Springs of Poetry," *New Republic,* 5 Dec. 1923, 8. Quotations that follow are from this essay.

2. Eliot, *Essays,* 10.

3. "Les Fenêtres," *Mallarmé,* 17.

4. Hartley, introduction, *Mallarmé,* ix. The declaration came in Mallarmé's letter to his good friend Henri Cazalis as he began "Hérodiade."

VI. "A Labor of Tears": *Dark Summer* (1929)

1. Elder Olsen, "Louise Bogan and Léonie Adams," *Chicago Review* 8 (Fall 1954), 74.

2. H.D., *Bid Me to Live* (New York: Grove Press, 1960), 136.

3. Ridgeway, "The Poetry of Louise Bogan," Ph.D. diss., University of California, Riverside, 87–88. The citation comes from Box XIII, Folder 3, Bogan Papers.

4. Ridgeway, *Bogan,* 62.

5. L. W. Dodd, "Four American Poets," *Yale Review* 19 (1930), 390.

VII. "Alone and Strong in My Peace": *The Sleeping Fury* (1937)

Epigraph: Arthur S. Wensinger and Carole Clew Hoey, ed. and trans., *Paula Modersohn-Becker: The Letters and Journals* (New York: Taplinger, 1983) 281.

1. Sandra Cookson writes, "The blackened stubble which remains after the fire has burned itself out is a recurring image in these early poems, and signifies the woman's sexuality depleted by the fires of passion." See her essay "The Repressed Becomes the Poem: Landscape and Quest in Two Poems by Louise Bogan" in *Critical Essays,* 194–203.

2. Helene Deutsch, "The Significance of Masochism in the Mental Life of Women," *The Psychoanalytic Reader,* ed. R. Fleiss (New York: International Universities Press, 1948), 231.

3. William Jay Smith, "Louise Bogan: A Woman's Words," *Critical Essays,* 117.

4. Karen Horney, "The Overvaluation of Love," *Feminine Psychology* (New York: W. W. Norton, 1967), 183.

5. Horney, *Feminine Psychology,* 184.

6. Frank, *Portrait,* 247.

7. Elizabeth Frank thinks that gossip about her twenties affair with John Coffey kept surfacing. See *Portrait,* 43–45.

8. Eda Lou Walton, review of *The Sleeping Fury, Nation* 24 (1937), 488. Reprinted in *Critical Essays,* 39–40.

9. Maxwell, "Louise Bogan's Story," 75–76.

10. Box XI, Folder 15, Bogan Papers, Amherst College Library.

11. Box XI, Folders 46–53, Bogan Papers.

12. Elizabeth Frank writes, "By the fall of 1934 she had separated for good from the poet Raymond Holden, whom she had married in 1925 and whose chronic lying had in large measure brought about her recent depression. See "Putting to Sea (Louise Bogan in 1936)," *Grand Street* 2.1 (1982), 132.

13. Box XI, Folder 59, Bogan Papers.

14. Olsen, *Silences*, 145.

15. William Butler Yeats, "The Choice," *Selected Poems*, 131.

16. Box XI, Folder 63, Bogan Papers.

17. Box XI, Folder 27, Bogan Papers.

18. Charles Baudelaire, "Le Voyage," *Baudelaire*, ed. Francis Scarfe (Baltimore: Penguin, 1964), 190. Translation mine.

19. Box XI, Folder 66, Bogan Papers.

20. The passage is from Otto Fenichel's *Outline of Clinical Psychoanalysis* and is quoted by Elizabeth Frank in her essay "Putting to Sea," 141.

21. Box XI, Folder 62, Bogan Papers.

22. Elizabeth Frank, "A Doll's Heart: The Girl in the Poetry of Edna St. Vincent Millay and Louise Bogan," *Critical Essays*, 146.

23. Sara Teasdale, "In a Darkening Garden," *Mirror of the Heart*, 120.

VIII. "This Light Is Loss Backward": *Poems and New Poems* (1941) and *Collected Poems 1923–1953* (1954)

Epigraphs: Marina Cvataeva, quoted by Tillie Olsen, in *Silences*, 145. "Four Quarters," Box XI, Folder 18, Bogan Papers.

1. Maxwell, "Louise Bogan's Story," 76.

2. Sarton, *World of Light*, 227.

3. Carolyn Heilbrun, introduction, *Mrs. Stevens Hears the Mermaids Singing*, by May Sarton (New York: W. W. Norton, 1965), xi.

4. Frank, "Putting to Sea," 131.

5. Marianne Moore, review of *Poems and New Poems*, *Nation*, 15 Nov. 1941, 486. Reprinted in *Critical Essays*, 61.

6. Malcolm Cowley, "Three Poets," *New Republic* 105 (1941), 625. Reprinted in *Critical Essays*, 58.

7. Babette Deutsch, review of *Poems and New Poems*, *New York Herald Tribune Books*, 28 Dec. 1941, 8. Reprinted in *Critical Essays*, 59.

8. Marie Collins, introduction, *Critical Essays*, 9.

9. Cather, born in 1873, was thus fifty-nine when Bogan met her. She and Bogan both lived to be seventy-three. Between 1930 and 1932, Cather went to Europe, lost her mother, published three short stories and a novel, moved and faced the serious illness of the woman she most loved, Isabelle McClung. See Phyllis C. Robinson, *Willa: The Life of Willa Cather* (New York: Holt, Rinehart and Winston, 1984), especially 254–68.

10. Edmund Wilson, "Justice to Edith Wharton," *Edith Wharton: A Collection of Critical Essays*, ed. Irving Howe (Englewood Cliffs, N.J.: Prentice-Hall, 1962), 27–28.

11. Box XI, Folder 72, Bogan Papers.

12. Box XI, Folder 70, Bogan Papers.

13. "The Catalpa Tree" was published in *Voices: A Quarterly of Poetry* Sept.-Dec. 1941, 8. I am indebted to Jaqueline Ridgeway for finding this poem. See her book, 107.

14. Yeats, *Selected Poems*, 96, 170.

15. Collins, introduction, *Critical Essays*, 11.

16. John Ciardi, review of *Collected Poems, 1923–53*, *Nation*, 22 May 1954, 445–45. Reprinted in *Critical Essays*, 66–67.

IX. "Now I Am Not Sure": *The Blue Estuaries: Poems 1923–1968* (1968)

Epigraph: David Plante, "Jean," *Difficult Women: A Memoir of Three* (New York: E. P. Dutton, 1983), 22.

1. Louise Bogan, "Notes to 'July Dawn,' " *Poems in Folio* (San Francisco/Mill Valley: Press of the Morning Sun, 1957).
2. Box XIX, Folder 1, Bogan Papers.
3. Elizabeth Frank says that a draft of "Masked Woman's Song" was sent to Edmund Wilson in November 1937. See *Portrait*, 406.
4. Ruth Limmer, "Circumscriptions," *Critical Essays*, 166–174.
5. Louise Bogan, "The Springs of Poetry," *New Republic*, 5 Dec. 1923, 8.

Conclusion: Redefining Literary Modernism

Epigraphs: Marianne Moore, *The Complete Poems* (New York: Macmillan, 1981), 91 (This is the last poem of *Selected Poems*, 1935.) Meridel LeSueur, reading, University of California, Berkeley, 3 Nov. 1981. Adrienne Rich, "The Trees," *Necessities of Life* (New York: W. W. Norton, 1966), 15. Audre Lorde, "Prologue," *Chosen Poems—Old and New* (New York: W. W. Norton, 1982), 58.

1. I am indebted to William Drake for aspects of this formulation. His forthcoming book from Macmillan, *Now I Become Myself,* will examine friendship and relationship as sources of empowerment for American women poets from 1912 through 1940.
2. John Crowe Ransom's reviews of Edna St. Vincent Millay are classics of this genre. See "The Poet as Woman," *Southern Review* 2 (1937), 783–806.
3. Louise Bogan, quoted by Ridgeway, *Bogan,* 20. The remarks were originally published in an essay called "Poetry" in *America Now*, ed. Harold E. Stearns (New York: Charles Scribner's Sons, 1938), 55.
4. I am indebted to Colette Patt for conversations, and a senior honors thesis, which elucidate this point.
5. See, for example, Ronald Bush, *T. S. Eliot: A Study in Character and Style* (Oxford: Oxford University Press, 1984); Milton J. Bates, *Wallace Stevens: A Mythology of Self* (Berkeley: University of California Press, 1985); Sandra Gilbert, "Costumes of the Mind: Transvestism as Metaphor in Modern Literature," *Writing and Sexual Difference,* ed. Elizabeth Abel (Chicago: University of Chicago Press, 1982), 193–219; *Lyric Poetry: Beyond the New Criticism,* ed. Chaviva Hosek and Patricia Parker (Ithaca: Cornell University Press, 1985).
6. Marianne De Koven notes that Eliot, Pound, Yeats, and Stevens were all political reactionaries. Her paper on "The Politics of Modernist Form" was presented in the session on "Rethinking the Politics of Early Modernism," MLA Convention, Chicago, 28 Dec. 1985. Sandra Gilbert and Susan Gubar, in their introduction to "modernism" from a feminist perspective, list all those relatively neglected writers, women and men, who countered these tendencies. See their *Norton Anthology of Literature by Women: The Tradition in English* (New York: W. W. Norton, 1985), 1225.
7. For a perspective on those black women poets who were writing at the same time as Bogan, see *Black Sister: Poetry by Black American Women, 1746–1980,* ed. Erlene Stetson (Bloomington: Indiana University Press, 1981) and Gloria T. Hull, "Black Women Poets from Wheatley to Walker," *Sturdy Black Bridges: Visions of Black Women in Literature,* ed. Roseann P. Bell, Bettye J. Parker, and Beverly Guy-Sheftall (Garden City, N.Y.: Doubleday, 1979), 69–86.
8. And this despite the eulogies at her death. W. H. Auden said in a commemorative tribute: "By temperament she was not a euphoric character and in her life she had much to endure. What, aside from their technical excellence, is most impressive about her

poems is the unflinching courage with which she faced her problems, her determination never to surrender to self-pity, but to wrest beauty and joy out of dark places. It was a privilege to have known her" (Maxwell, "Louise Bogan's Story," 76). *The New York Times* obituary, with the headline "Louise Bogan, Noted Poet Who Wrote About Love, Dead," called her "one of the most distinguished lyric poets in the English language" (5 Feb. 1970, 39). On the last page of its April 1970 issue, *Poetry* (126:58) chose a simple and elegant commemorative:

LOUISE BOGAN
1897–1970

Words made of breath, these also are undone.
And greedy sight abolished in its claim.
Light fails from ruin and from wall the same;
The loud sound and pure silence fall as one.
(from "Sonnet," 41)

SELECTED BIBLIOGRAPHY

Works by Louise Bogan

I. Poetry

Body of This Death. New York: Robert M. McBride, 1923.
Dark Summer. New York: Charles Scribner's Sons, 1929.
The Sleeping Fury. New York: Charles Scribner's Sons, 1937.
Poems and New Poems. New York: Charles Scribner's Sons, 1941.
Collected Poems, 1923–1953. New York: Noonday Press, 1954.
The Blue Estuaries: Poems 1923–1968. New York: Farrar, Straus & Giroux, 1968.

II. Criticism

Achievement in American Poetry, 1900–1950. Chicago: Henry Regnery, 1951.
Selected Criticism: Poetry and Prose. New York: Noonday Press, 1955.
A Poet's Alphabet: Reflections on the Literary Art and Vocation, ed. Robert Phelps and
   Ruth Limmer. New York: McGraw-Hill, 1970.

III. Letters and Memoirs

What the Woman Lived: Selected Letters of Louise Bogan, 1920–1970, ed. Ruth
   Limmer. New York: Harcourt Brace Jovanovich, 1973.
Journey Around My Room: The Autobiography of Louise Bogan, A Mosaic, ed. Ruth
   Limmer. New York: The Viking Press, 1980.

IV. Articles and Suppressed Poems

"A Letter." *Body of This Death.* New York: Robert M. McBride, 1923. 5–7.
"Decoration." *Body of This Death.* 2.
"Epitaph for a Romantic Woman." *Body of This Death.* 18.
"Elders," " Resolve," "Leave-taking," "To A Dead Lover." *Poetry* 20 (1922): 248–51.
"From the Journals of a Poet." *New Yorker,* 30 Jan. 1978, 39–70.
"For An Old Dance." *New Yorker,* 1 Feb. 1930, 17.
"Gift." *New Yorker,* 28 May 1932, 20.
"Pyrotechnics." *Liberator* 6, no. 5 (May 1932): 14.
"Song." *Body of This Death.* 25.
"Survival." *Measure* 9 (Nov. 1921): 5.
"The Catalpa Tree." *Voices: A Quarterly of Poetry* (Sept-Dec. 1941): 8.
"The Notebooks of Louise Bogan (1935–36.)" *Antaeus* 27 (Autumn 1977): 120–29.
"The Springs of Poetry." *New Republic,* 5 Dec. 1923, 8.
"The Young Wife." *Others* 4 (Dec. 1917): 11–13.
"Women." Pasadena: Ward Ritchie Press, 1929.
"Words for Departure." *Body of This Death.* 10–11.

Works about Louise Bogan

Bowles, Gloria. "Suppression and Expression in Poetry by American Women: Louise
   Bogan, Denise Levertov and Adrienne Rich." Ph.D. diss. University of Califor-
   nia, Berkeley, 1976.
———. "The Pursuit of Perfection." *Women's Review of Books.* July 1985: 8–9.

Collins, Marie, ed. *Critical Essays on Louise Bogan.* Boston: G. K. Hall, 1984.
Cookson, Sandra. " 'All Has Been Translated Into Treasure': The Art of Louise
    Bogan." Ph.D. diss. University of Connecticut, 1980.
Couchman, Jane. "Louise Bogan: A Bibliography of Primary and Secondary Materials,
    1915–1975." *Bulletin of Bibliography* 33, no. 2 (Feb.-Mar. 1976): 73–77, 104:
    no. 3 (April-June 1976); 111–26, 147; and no. 3 (July-Sept. 1976): 178–81.
Frank, Elizabeth. *Louise Bogan: A Portrait.* New York: Knopf, 1985.
Goldfein, R. Phyllis. "Words She Always Knew: A Consideration of Louise Bogan and
    Her Poetry." *Moving Out* 7.2 (1978): 73–77.
Middlebrook, Diane. "Liberation: Poetry of William Butler Yeats and Louise Bogan."
    Worlds Into Words: Understanding Modern Poems. New York: W. W. Norton,
    1978. 47–63.
Moldaw, Carol Ann. "The Double Dream: Order and Emotion in the Poetry of Louise
    Bogan." B. A. thesis Harvard University, 1979.
Ridgeway, Jaqueline. *Louise Bogan.* Boston: Twayne Publishers, 1984.
———. "The Poetry of Louise Bogan." Ph.D. diss. University of California, Riverside,
    1977.
Sarton, May. "Louise Bogan." *A World of Light.* New York: W. W. Norton, 1976.
    215–34.
Smith, William Jay. "Louise Bogan: A Woman's Words." *The Streaks of the Tulip:
    Selected Criticism.* New York: Seymour Lawrence/Delacorte, 1972. 31–56.

General Works

De Shazer, Mary K. *Inspiring Women: Re-Imagining the Muse.* New York: Pergamon,
    1986.
Drake, William, ed. *Mirror of the Heart: Poems of Sara Teasdale.* New York: Macmil-
    lan, 1984.
Friedman, Susan Stanford. *Psyche Reborn: The Emergence of H.D.* Bloomington:
    Indiana University Press, 1981.
Gilbert, Sandra M., and Susan Gubar. *The Madwoman in the Attic: The Woman
    Writer and the Nineteenth-Century Literary Imagination.* New Haven: Yale
    University Press, 1979.
———. *Shakespeare's Sisters: Feminist Essays on Women Poets.* Bloomington: Indiana
    University Press, 1979.
Gregory, Horace and Zaturenska, Marya. *A History of American Poetry 1900–1940.*
    New York: Harcourt Brace, 1942.
Howe, Florence and Ellen Bass, eds. *No More Masks!: An Anthology of Poems by
    Women.* Garden City: Doubleday Anchor, 1973.
Juhasz, Suzanne. *Naked and Fiery Forms.* New York: Harper & Row, 1976.
Middlebrook, Diane, and Marilyn Yalom, eds. *Coming to Light: American Women
    Poets in the Twentieth Century.* Ann Arbor: University of Michigan Press, 1985.
Olsen, Tillie. *Silences.* New York: Delacorte Press/Seymour Lawrence, 1965.
Ostriker, Alicia. *Writing Like A Woman.* Ann Arbor: University of Michigan Press, 1983.
Riding, Laura and Robert Graves. *A Survey of Modernist Poetry.* London: William
    Heinemann, 1929.
Showalter, Elaine, ed. *These Modern Women.* Old Westbury, N.Y.: Feminist Press,
    1978.
Sproat, Elaine, ed. " 'Women and the Creative Will': A Lecture by Lola Ridge, 1919."
    Michigan Occasional Papers in Women's Studies 28 (1981).
Walker, Cheryl. *The Nightingale's Burden: Women Poets and American Culture before
    1900.* Bloomington: Indiana University Press, 1982.
———. "The Women's Tradition in Poetry." Ph.D. diss. Brandeis University, 1973.
Wilson, Edmund. *Letters on Literature and Politics, 1912–72.* Ed. Elena Wilson. New
    York: Farrar, Straus and Giroux, 1977.

INDEX